James Cuno, Paul Goldberger, and Joseph Rosa, with a photographic portfolio by Judith Turner
Architectural photography by Paul Warchol
The Art Institute of Chicago and Yale University Press, New Haven and London

THE MODERN WING RENZO PIANO AND THE ART INSTITUTE OF CHICAGO

CONTENTS

FOREWORD

A BUILDING OF ANY SIZE and importance takes years to plan and construct and involves hundreds of people working together to make it possible. This level of cooperation, together with the building's programmatic contribution to the life of the institution it serves, is the most rewarding aspect of any such project. The new Modern Wing of the Art Institute of Chicago began in the autumn of 1998, when then director and president James N. Wood proposed an addition that was principally to provide gallery space for the display of South Asian and contemporary art. Early in January 1999, Renzo Piano visited the museum for the first time, and in March of that year his appointment as architect of the addition was approved by the Art Institute's Board of Trustees.

Wood and Piano struggled with the original site for this proposed addition—the area south of Gunsaulus Hall over the current electric railway commuter lines—and its intended connections to the museum's Morton Wing and Rice Building. At the same time, however, the Goodman Theatre had announced that it was vacating its facility on the northeast corner of the Art Institute's site, just across the street from what was then being called Lakefront Millennium Project, plans for which were beginning to take shape. With the departure of the Goodman Theatre in 2000, the Art Institute moved its building project to that location—a shift that enabled Wood and Piano to rethink the new building's program. An education center and galleries for architecture and classic modern art were added, and over the next two years the project grew from 70,000 square feet to 265,000 square feet. Meanwhile, Frank Gehry's arresting design for the Pritzker Pavilion in Millennium Park caused Piano to acknowledge the inevitable link between the new Art Institute building and the park. In the fall of 2003, with the museum project by then in construction drawings, Jim Wood announced his retirement from the Art Institute. He had worked on the addition for five years, first under Chairman of the Board of Trustees John D. Nichols and then under his successor, John H. Bryan. A committee to oversee the construction of the project had been formed with trustee Andrew Rosenfield as chairman, while another for the Building of the Century Campaign was hard at work with trustee Louis B. Susman as chairman.

I was hired to succeed Wood early in 2004 and assumed my duties in September of that year. The building project was well underway, but we had not yet been given approval by the Board of Trustees to break ground. Over the course of the next six months, with Millennium Park open and an obvious success, we revisited certain aspects of our project. We removed South Asian and Islamic art from their designated galleries and in their place planned a special-exhibitions gallery for modern and contemporary art, introduced galleries for photography, increased the scope of architecture to include design, relocated a "black box" gallery for video and new-media presentations, and changed the garden from one experienced only from outside the building to one experienced internally. We also added a third floor to the project's west pavilion to provide space for a restaurant and an outdoor sculpture terrace. These we connected to Millennium Park by way of a dramatic pedestrian bridge that would soar over Monroe Street. This proved to be a bold stroke: the elegant Nichols Bridgeway—named in honor of John Nichols and his wife, Alexandra, who had succeeded him on our Board of Trustees—was designed to integate the museum with the park, and it instantly captured the public's imagination. It announced our intentions to make the addition, which would soon officially be named the Modern Wing, a significant civic building with its own front door onto a major public venue.

With the design complete, we received approval from the Board of Trustees to break ground and did so on May 31, 2005. Over the next four years we worked closely with the Renzo Piano Building Workshop; the project's architect of record, Interactive Design, Inc.; and the construction manager, Turner Construction Company, to realize the building, which opened on May 16, 2009. At the same time, we went back into our historic building and renovated and reinstalled many galleries, significantly changing the installation of European paintings and sculpture and creating new galleries for European decorative arts and South Asian sculpture. Ironically, the latter was installed where this entire project had begun. For it was the gift of the James and Marilynn Alsdorf Collection of Indian, Himalayan, and Southeast Asian Art in 1997 that propelled Jim Wood to conceive of an addition in the first place. When we opened the new Alsdorf Galleries in Gunsaulus Hall in December 2008, with new windows opened north onto the Modern Wing and Millennium Park, we were acknowledging the full history of the project. Such has been the nature of this project: we ended where we began and broke new ground for the museum along the way.

Throughout the ten years of the project, every curatorial department in the museum got involved, as, of course, did all of our conservators, registrars, security and visitor services personnel, and our administrative, financial, and legal staff. While the entire staff of 2005 through 2009 is acknowledged elsewhere in this book, I should especially note a few individuals whose contributions to the project were fundamental to its success. First of all, of course, and for obvious reasons, there is James N. Wood, who served this institution with distinction for twenty-four years. He was helped in the conception of the project by Deputy Director Neal Benezra, who also served as head of the Department of Modern and Contemporary Art and is now director of the San Francisco Museum of Modern Art; Calvert Audrain, Vice President for Operations; and Robert Jones, Director of Design and Construction. Patricia Woodworth, who was hired in 2001 as Executive Vice President for Finance and Administration/CFO, and Meredith Mack, Senior Vice President for Finance and Operations, managed much of the business of the project, including staffing the trustees' Modern Wing Oversight Committee, which, as its title suggests, exercised official review of the building's progress. At that same time, Edward W. Horner, Jr., Executive Vice President for Development and Public Affairs, led the museum's fund-raising campaign, working closely with consultant James F. Feldstein of Charles Feldstein & Company.

During this whole period, trustee leadership was crucial. Chairman John Nichols first encouraged Jim Wood to develop the project; his successor, John Bryan, led the museum's board through the decision to break ground and add significantly to the project's scope; Bryan in turn was succeeded as Chairman of the Board of Trustees by Thomas J. Pritzker, who brought the Modern Wing to its opening. Tom Pritzker was aided in this by trustee Andrew Rosenfield, who chaired the Oversight Committee, and, especially in the end, by committee member Steven Crown. John Bryan also worked closely with Louis Susman to lead our fund-raising efforts, bringing together numerous volunteers to raise more than $400 million in the end. The extraordinary generosity of our donors—hundreds of them, whether private, corporate, or foundations—was historic in scale. Never before had this museum mounted a capital campaign of more than $60 million. These donors, too, are individually recognized later in this book.

As things happen, museum leadership of the project changed over the course of time. In January 2007, Ed Horner left and was succeeded by Mary Jane Drews as the museum's Vice President for Development. Patricia Woodworth left in November 2007 to work at the J. Paul Getty Trust, where she rejoined Jim Wood, who had assumed the presidency of the trust earlier that year. After an administrative restructuring, Meredith Mack was promoted to Deputy Director and Chief Operating Officer and assumed principal oversight of the building project.

Increasingly over the next three years, Douglas Druick, Searle Chair of Medieval through Modern European Painting and Sculpture; Stephanie D'Alessandro, Gary C. and Frances Comer Curator of Modern Painting and Sculpture; James Rondeau, Frances and Thomas Dittmer Chair of Contemporary Art; Joseph Rosa, John H. Bryan Chair of Architecture and Design; Zoë Ryan, Neville Bryan Curator of Design; Chair of Photography David Travis, who in 2008 was succeeded by Matthew Witkovsky; and Robert Eskridge, the Woman's Board Endowed Executive Director of Museum Education, worked closely with Joost Moolhuijzen, Carolyn Maxwell-Mahon, and Dominique Rat, architects from the Renzo Piano Building Project, to design the inaugural gallery installations and fill out the new Ryan Education Center. Naturally, Joost, Carolyn, and Dominique worked very closely on every aspect of the project over its many years. In this they were joined by Robert Larsen, Charles G. Young, and Dina Griffin of Interactive Design, and by Leif Selkregg, Barry Quinn, Bridget Bush, and Rick Watson of the Rise Group, our project managers on the job.

Working closely with the curators were Frank Zuccari, Grainger Executive Director of Conservation, and the entire staff of our many conservation labs, as well as Carrie Heinonen, Vice President for Marketing, and Erin Hogan, Director of Public Affairs, who with their staff planned the marketing and opening of the building. Equally critical to the Modern Wing's successful opening was the good work of Julia E. Getzels, Executive Vice President, General Counsel and Secretary; Michelle Lehrman Jenness, Associate Vice President for Protection Services; William Caddick, Associate Vice President for Physical Plant; Bernice Chu, Associate Vice President for Design and Construction; Elizabeth Grainer, Vice President for Auxiliary Operations; Sam Quigley, Vice President for Collections Management, Imaging, and Information Technology; Dorothy Schroeder, Vice President for Exhibitions and Museum Administration; and Jeanne Ladd, Vice President for Museum Finance. The documentation of the project and its presentation in this book is the product of the good work of our Publications Department, especially Executive Director Robert V. Sharp and Director Sarah E. Guernsey. I am also especially grateful to Paul Goldberger, Judith Turner, and Paul Warchol for their incisive and creative contributions to this volume.

Finally, I want to recognize the vision, professional skills, and acute aesthetic and personal sensitivities of our architect, Renzo Piano. Renzo is one of our era's greatest architects and without question, the leading museum architect of our time. Inheriting this project from Jim Wood and collaborating with Renzo—and the Board of Trustees, our donors, and my colleagues—to realize the Modern Wing have proved to be an extraordinary opportunity. That we did it successfully, while simultaneously enhancing the role of the Art Institute in the civic and cultural life of Chicago, has been the dream of a professional lifetime.

James Cuno
President and Eloise W. Martin Director
The Art Institute of Chicago

CONSTRUCTING
THE MODERN WING
2005-2009

Opposite page and top
From the drilling of 60-foot-deep shafts for the foundation of the Modern Wing in the fall of 2005, through the erection of the structural steel framework of the west pavilion during the summer of 2007, to the installation of heating coils for the open-air terrace in the late fall of 2008, the construction of the Modern Wing spanned four full years and represents the largest expansion of the Art Institute of Chicago ever undertaken.

Top and left
Lying between the three-story structures on either side of it, the two-story-high, 300-foot-long Griffin Court is the "main street" of the Modern Wing. With the new entrance on Monroe Street at its north end and a connection to McKinlock Court at its south, this grand, skylit space, crowned with a elegant series of cabled trusses, creates a new north–south axis for the museum.

Opposite page
One of the principal features of the Modern Wing—positioned at the midpoint of the Griffin Court on its east side—is the steel-framed, oak-clad suspended staircase that provides access to the galleries above.

Above, left and right
The nearly 50-foot-wide, clear-span bays of the east pavilion of the Modern Wing are constructed with precast concrete beams and oversized panes in the glass curtain wall exterior.

Above, left and right
The third-floor galleries of the east pavilion are covered with a skylight composed of ultraviolet-filtering glass. Hanging below the skylight are lightweight fabric panels that further soften the light in the galleries and create the ceiling in those rooms.

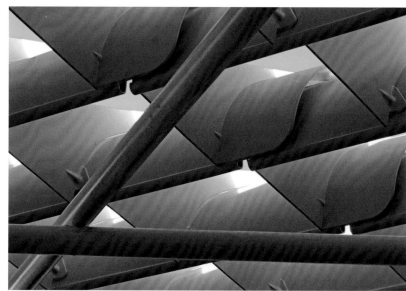

Opposite page and above
Once the glass roof over the third floor of the east pavilion was completed in September 2007, the installation of base framework of the "flying carpet," the signal feature of the Modern Wing, could begin. In February and March 2008, from a storage yard set up along Columbus Drive, individual units of "blades" were brought up into position and secured to this support structure.

Left
Covering the entire east pavilion and extending over the Monroe Street façade and the Pritzker Garden south of the building, the 2,656 blades that compose the "flying carpet" constitute a massive, 225-foot-square sunscreen that prevents direct sunlight from striking the third-floor skylights but allows reflected light to illuminate the galleries below.

Opposite page
Following the groundbreaking for the Nichols Bridgeway in September 2007, fabrication of the individual steel sections proceeded off-site, while preparations to cantilever the bridge off the west side of the building continued. In late April 2008 the first pieces of its 15-foot-wide hull were hoisted into place.

Top and above
Large temporary platforms and scaffolds held the sections of the bridge in place so that the steel could be welded together. Over the following months, the Nichols Bridgeway was extended north toward its termination deep inside Millennium Park.

FACING THE CHALLENGE BUILDING THE MODERN WING JAMES CUNO

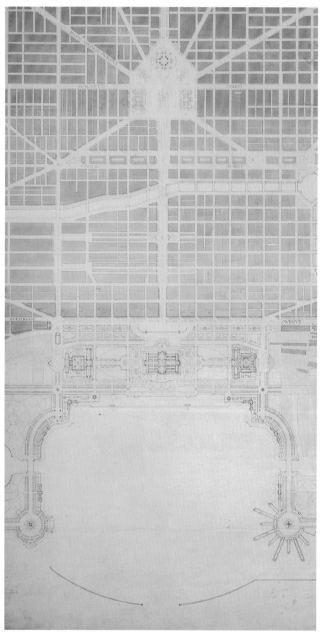

THE ART INSTITUTE OF CHICAGO has been located in Grant Park for more than 115 years, although few visitors realize that all of the land that the museum sits on is man-made, just as most of the area that now constitutes Grant Park was originally under lake water (fig. 1).[1] Indeed, the Art Institute's building on Michigan Avenue was erected on land filled with the rubble from the Great Chicago Fire of 1871, but as more parkland was created during the 1890s east of the railway tracks that lie immediately behind the museum's 1893 building, that property was soon littered with stables, squatters' shacks, garbage, and debris. In 1906 Chicago architect Daniel H. Burnham was commissioned to develop a plan for the city, which, when published in 1909, addressed everything from transportation to streets to slum removal. Coauthored with Edward H. Bennett, Burnham's *Plan of Chicago* also called for the recreational development of the lakefront with a series of parks and lagoons stretching from Jackson Park on the South Side to Wilmette, beyond Chicago to the north.[2]

Central to his lakefront plan was Grant Park, which Burnham conceived as the intellectual and cultural hub of the city, with harmoniously designed buildings for the Field Museum (natural sciences) in the center, the Chicago Public Library (letters) to the south, and the Art Institute (fine arts) to the north (fig. 2). He also foresaw the Art Institute's need for expansion and proposed new buildings with open-air loggias and gardens. As examples of what he envisioned, Burnham cited the contemporary development of Boston's Museum of Fine Arts in the park along the Fenway and of the Metropolitan Museum of Art in New York's Central Park.

Burnham's plan for the city center would not be realized, however, in part because of a series of successful lawsuits filed over a twenty-year period by A. Montgomery Ward—head of one of the city's largest retailers—that called for the removal of structures in the park and forbade the construction of new buildings above grade.[3] The sole exception was the Art Institute, which had begun the construction of its Michigan Avenue building in 1891. The Chicago Public Library building, also begun in 1891, was situated outside the park on Michigan Avenue just north of the Art Institute; it would not relocate for another hundred years. The Field Museum would open in 1921 on land south of Grant Park donated by the Illinois Central Railroad. The Art Institute would eventually expand over the railway tracks in 1916 with the construction of Gunsaulus Hall (which is, strictly speaking, not on parkland) and subsequently in 1924 and 1925 by embedding its Hutchinson Wing, McKinlock Court, and Goodman Theatre *in* the park's landfill.

By the 1920s the park was complete but for parcels of land north of Monroe Street and east and west of Columbus Drive (originally called Grant Boulevard). The east parcel would become first a street-level parking lot in 1921 and in the mid-1970s a large, underground garage (fig. 3). The land above the garage was developed into Daley Bicentennial Plaza, named in honor of Mayor Richard J. Daley, who had died in December 1976. Almost simultaneously, a group of civic activists called for completing Grant Park by building over the railway yard west of Columbus Drive (directly north of the Art Institute) and developing a performance facility for the Grant Park Symphony Orchestra and other small performing groups in a garden setting. Called Lakefront Gardens, the project was endorsed by Mayor Michael Bilandic in 1977, and its optimistic proponents claimed it would be designed by 1978 and built by 1980. But it never generated broad public support, and in 1994, after decades of effort, and in the face of persistent political opposition and rising costs, Lakefront Gardens, Inc., the entity created to promote the garden plan, dissolved.[4]

The unfinished park remained a challenge for Mayor Richard M. Daley, who was first elected in 1989. Seeing it as the ideal city project to garner support marking the new millennium, he

figure 1 (opposite page, top)
The Art Institute of Chicago,
Michigan Avenue at Adams Street,
under construction, 1892/93.

figure 2 (opposite page)
Daniel H. Burnham and Edward
H. Bennett, plan of the proposed
redevelopment of the Chicago
lakefront and central business
district; plate 129 from *Plan of
Chicago* (1909). Drawing attributed
to Fernand Janin, c. 1908; graphite,
ink, and wash on paper; 170.2 x
89.9 cm. On permanent loan to the
Art Institute of Chicago from the
City of Chicago (25.148.1966).

figure 3
View of the lakefront, looking
southwest, over the construction
of the Richard J. Daley Bicentennial
Plaza atop the Monroe Street
underground garage, 1976. The
Art Institute and its new Columbus
Drive addition (completed in
1977) are visible in the upper
left corner.

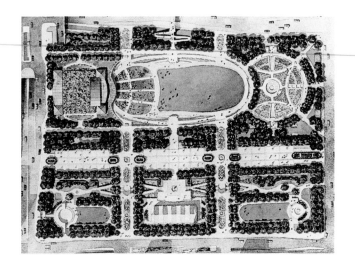

figure 4
Skidmore, Owings & Merrill, plan
of the proposed development
of Lakefront Millennium Project,
Chicago, 1998.

approached Adrian Smith of the Chicago-based architectural firm Skidmore, Owings & Merrill to develop preliminary plans, which eventually included an underground parking garage, gardens, public art, and a music pavilion (fig. 4). Daley announced his support for the Lakefront Millennium Project, as it was then called, in March 1998, and he named John H. Bryan, an important Art Institute trustee, to serve as chief fund-raiser for the park's all-important group of private donors. Having recently collaborated with Frank Gehry on the Guggenheim Museum in Bilbao, Spain, Adrian Smith suggested that Gehry might design something to adorn the proposed music pavilion. Bryan was immediately interested and encouraged Smith to approach him. When Smith suggested to Gehry that he design a sculpture for the pavilion's stage, perhaps a large glass fish such as he had done for the Walker Art Gallery Sculpture Park in Minneapolis in 1986, Gehry said he wasn't interested. Later that summer Cindy Pritzker, a noted Chicago philanthropist and the wife of Jay Pritzker, who together with her had established the Pritzker Architecture Prize, approached Bryan to say that if he were serious about involving Gehry, then he should be asked to design the pavilion itself and not just a decorative element for it. Six months later, when also invited to design a bridge from the new park across Columbus Drive to the Daley Bicentennial Plaza, Gehry agreed to design the pavilion—to which the Pritzker family pledged substantial support and which would subsequently be named in honor of Jay Pritzker. The site for this major new facility was on the eastern half of the park, across Monroe Street from the Art Institute.[5]

While all of this was going on north of Monroe Street, the chairman of the Art Institute's Board of Trustees, John D. Nichols, had asked James N. Wood, president and director of the museum, what he foresaw as the museum's greatest need. Since his arrival in 1980, Wood had vigorously renovated and expanded its galleries, engaging architect Thomas Beeby to undertake the 1988 addition of the Daniel F. and Ada L. Rice Building, located east of the railway tracks and south of Gunsaulus Hall.[6] In 1996, prompted by the impending departure of the Goodman Theatre from its building on Columbus Drive at Monroe Street, and with an eye on the city's long-range plans for Grant Park, the Art Institute had commissioned Skidmore, Owings & Merrill to prepare a development analysis for the full build-out of its site (figs. 5–6).[7] With SOM's analysis in hand, Wood knew of greater development potential for the Art Institute site, and he proposed adding a wing to house its important and poorly presented collections of modern and contemporary art; the arts of Africa and Pre-Columbian America; and those of India, the Himalayas, and Southeast Asia. Encouraged by Nichols, Wood approached Renzo Piano in November 1998 to gauge his interest in the potential project. Two months later—only weeks after Frank Gehry had accepted the commission for the music pavilion—Piano traveled to Chicago (during a true Chicago blizzard) to learn more about Wood's thoughts for the Art Institute's expansion.[8]

By then, Wood and his colleagues had developed thoughts about a 70,000-square-foot "New South Building" that would lie south of Gunsaulus Hall—spanning the railroad tracks and connecting the Morton Wing on the west side of the tracks with the Rice Building to the east—as well as a 30,000-square-foot garden deck facing Jackson Boulevard. The building was to contain three levels, with galleries for Indian and Southeast Asian as well as African and Pre-Columbian art on the first level; galleries for later twentieth-century art on the second; and on the third, conference/meeting rooms and possibly a café with access to a rooftop terrace or a single, large dining area. Art storage was also considered for an undetermined location. Importantly, there was to be no public access to the garden. The building was intended principally to provide much-needed gallery spaces (46,000 square feet over two floors) and improve circulation within the museum by bridging existing wings.

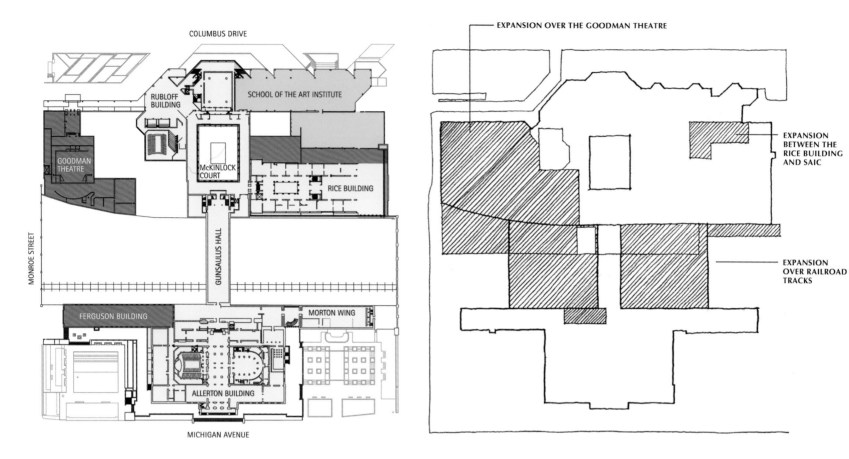

COLUMBUS DRIVE

EXPANSION OVER THE GOODMAN THEATRE

COLUMBUS DRIVE

RUBLOFF BUILDING

SCHOOL OF THE ART INSTITUTE

GOODMAN THEATRE

McKINLOCK COURT

RICE BUILDING

MONROE STREET

GUNSAULUS HALL

FERGUSON BUILDING

MORTON WING

ALLERTON BUILDING

MICHIGAN AVENUE

EXPANSION BETWEEN THE RICE BUILDING AND SAIC

EXPANSION OVER RAILROAD TRACKS

figure 5
Overall site plan of the Art
Institute of Chicago, 1996.

figure 6
Skidmore, Owings & Merrill,
plan of the Art Institute showing
potential areas of expansion;
from *The Art Institute of Chicago:
Future Site Development and
Master Plan* (Chicago, June 1996).

While interested in the project, Piano was convinced that it needed to be part of a larger, integrated plan for the entire museum site. A month after his visit, he wrote to Wood that he was "very pleased to learn that you see the necessity of a general Concept Design for the entire museum area. I still believe, following my visit and our conversations [January 4–6, 1999], that you need to establish a general vision at the urban scale (as well as, of course, at the functional and cultural level). You need to give 'unity' to the entire complex in the general 'diversity' so well expressing the museum's growth and history. My feeling is that by solving the connection across the railways, you need a Piazza or a Courtyard that may become a self-orienting centre of gravity."[9] Piano saw that the museum needed more than additional galleries. It needed also to provide its visitors with a more coherent experience, a "magical" gathering space from which one could choose to go off into a particular gallery, lecture hall, activity space, or restaurant. Through decades of growth on both sides of the railway tracks, but for the most part south of Gunsaulus Hall, the museum had lost the center it once had before these additions compromised the clarity of the original 1893 Beaux-Arts plan. The museum had become a cluster of cul-de-sacs divided east and west by a two-story, windowless gallery building.

Over the next few months, while Wood and Piano continued their discussions, the museum contacted numerous other architects—local, national, and international—and inquired of their interest in the project. Of those who were ultimately interviewed, the clear first choice of the museum's administration was the Renzo Piano Building Workshop, and at a meeting on February 26, 1999, the Board of Trustees' Committee on Buildings and Grounds agreed to recommend to the full board that it hire Piano to provide site analysis and schematic design services relative to the proposed south building and garden project. A week later, on March 8, the trustees

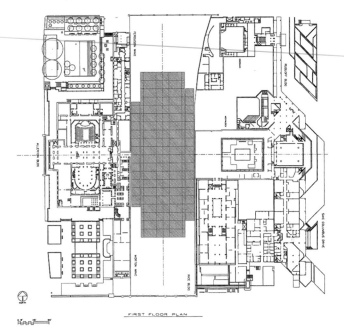

figure 7
Renzo Piano Building Workshop,
plan of a proposed addition to
the Art Institute, May 14, 1999.

FIRST FLOOR PLAN

unanimously approved the committee's recommendation, which the museum announced to the press the following day.

A few months later, in the Art Institute's *Annual Report* for that fiscal year, Wood reflected on the museum's choice of Piano and the importance of the project for the institution's future, clearly acknowledging the relevance of the Lakefront Millennium Project to his conception of the museum's plans: "For much of the past year, we have been focused on what the Art Institute could and should be beyond the year 2000. Architecture is essential to the civic identity and functional success of the museum. Our collections and programs have grown beyond the capacity of our present buildings, and the ambitious public works transforming the parkland around us present a unique opportunity to contribute to the enhancement of the very heart of our city. With this in mind, . . . we have engaged Italian architect Renzo Piano to help us define the Art Institute's future needs and design a building that will enhance the experience of our collections, while stating clearly our commitment as an institution for and of the twenty-first century."[10] Over the next four years, as Piano worked with the Art Institute to design the new addition, Millennium Park and its Gehry-designed music pavilion would exert considerable influence over Piano's design.

Selecting Piano was a bold stroke. Not only was he regarded by many as one of the world's leading architects—having been awarded the Pritzker Prize the previous year—but he was generally regarded as the best museum architect of his generation. His earlier U.S. museum projects, the Menil Collection (1987) and Cy Twombly Gallery (1995) in Houston, were greatly admired by architects and compared to Louis Kahn's Kimbell Museum for their elegantly proportioned, light-filled galleries and their sensitive siting within parklands. And his most recent work in this vein, the Beyeler Foundation Museum (1997) in Basel, Switzerland, was thought to be the elegant alternative to Gehry's recently opened and expressively baroque Guggenheim Museum Bilbao. Piano was also the Art Institute's first non-Chicago-based architect since Shepley, Rutan and Coolidge of Boston designed the 1893 building. The museum's other architects, especially Skidmore, Owings & Merrill, were of course internationally active, but they did not have the celebrated profile of a Pritzker Prize winner. And with Frank Gehry (himself a Pritzker Prize laureate in 1989) at work on the nearby music pavilion; with Cesar Pelli and Ricardo Legoretta creating buildings at the University of Chicago (soon to be joined by Rafael Viñoly, who would design the university's new Graduate School of Business); and with yet another Pritzker winner, Rem Koolhaas, undertaking a major building for the Illinois Institute of Technology, the international standing of the Art Institute's architect, while not a determining factor, was nonetheless important.[11]

Immediately upon learning of the board's unanimous decision, Piano began to assemble his design development group, to be led by Bernard Plattner and Joost Moolhuijzen. The two were dispatched to Chicago in the first days of April 1999 to meet the Art Institute's team. The first true "workshop" meetings were held in the Paris offices of the Renzo Piano Building Workshop on May 14–15. From the beginning the RPBW conceived of an addition to be built equally on both sides of Gunsaulus Hall (figs. 7–8). The AIC team, on the other hand, kept focusing on building only south of the tracks, with Gunsaulus Hall remaining the museum's axial spine, running east–west along the north end of the new building with a clear view through to McKinlock Court. At the third meeting, two months later on July 12, the architects proposed a new distribution of the collection galleries over four floors:

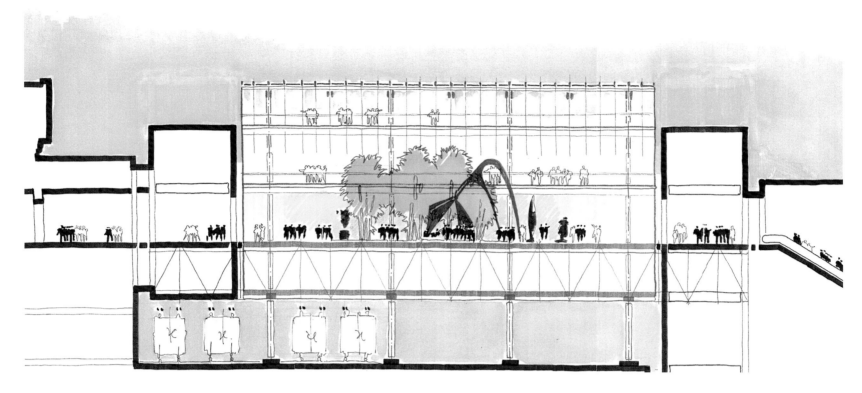

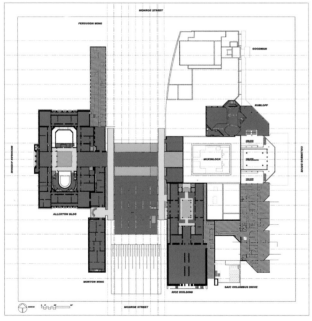

figure 8 (top)
RPBW, sectional view of a proposed addition to the Art Institute, May 14, 1999.

figure 9
RPBW, plan of a proposed addition to the Art Institute, July 12, 1999, with a reconstructed Gunsaulus Hall for Indian, Himalayan, and Southeast Asian art, and enclosed winter gardens north and south; additional galleries for 20th-century art.

Ground level: African, Pre-Columbian, and ancient Mediterranean arts east of the tracks connecting with the lower level of the Rice Building (American painting and sculpture court)

First floor: Indian, Himalayan, and Southeast Asian arts in new, double-height renovated galleries in what was previously Gunsaulus Hall, with glass-enclosed winter gardens on both the north and south sides, running the full extent of the galleries; contemporary art and modern art, south of the southern winter garden, connecting to the Morton Wing and Rice Building at their first-floor levels (this was complicated by a change in levels between Morton and Rice)

Second floor: Winter garden and sculpture court, accessed only from the galleries below

Third floor: Woman's Board meeting rooms[12]

This new scheme involved demolishing Gunsaulus Hall and constructing double-height galleries for Himalayan, Indian, and Southeast Asian art as a new symbolic center of the museum (referred to as the museum's "heart") (fig. 9). During that workshop, however, Wood urged the team to concentrate on only *renovating* and not *destroying* Gunsaulus Hall, and only building south of it, over the tracks. He also gave instructions for the gallery conditions he wanted for the different galleries:

Modern art (first half of the 20th century): Skylights, 15-foot ceiling height

Contemporary art (later 20th century): No need for skylights, 20-foot ceiling height

Asian art: Side lights, 15-foot ceiling height, adjacency to a winter garden

African and Pre-Columbian art: No natural light, 15-foot ceiling height

Architecture: Side lights with views out over the city, 15-foot ceiling height[13]

It was suggested that the African and Pre-Columbian galleries might not end up in the new building but could be installed in renovated galleries on the ground floor of the Morton Wing and that the second floor of the Morton Wing could be used for storage and/or temporary exhibition space. And it was mentioned that Museum Education might eventually go into a building on the site of the former Goodman Theatre.

Throughout these early sessions, Piano emphasized the poetics of the scheme, comparing the museum to a Tuscan village, like San Gimignano, combining sacred spaces (galleries) with profane ones (public, social spaces), allowing for the experience of a human-scaled village street. Wood responded that he didn't want a "Swiss watch like Beyeler" but something "more aristocratically restrained, more in keeping with Dominique de Menil's choice of simple pine floors." Piano proposed that the roof covering the building could rise up from lower floors to the center point over what was Gunsaulus Hall, and then eventually, when the museum built another addition north over the tracks, it would descend equally as on the south side "like a sculpture, very light, flying, like an umbrella." He also proposed leaving the roof open at the center point, covered with glass skylights to bring natural light down through velum laylights into what he still hoped would be a double cube, a so-called "Golden Box": "the most abstract place in the museum; a very calm, contemplative space" (fig. 10). And he suggested demolishing the Allerton Building's Grand Staircase because it was "too heavy." When Wood objected to this, Piano suggested making at least the central section of the Grand Staircase more transparent so that visitors to the museum could, upon entering the museum, see through the staircase down the main axis of the museum: the new galleries of Himalayan, Indian, and Southeast Asian arts.

From the beginning, Piano wanted to combine a new, reinforced main axis with, above, a dramatic, light-filled, "magical" volume. Wood, on the other hand, continued to focus only on the new building south of Gunsaulus Hall. He allowed for the possibility of additional building phases, but noted that they couldn't be determined at that time. He wrote to Piano on September 16, 1999: "My primary concern is that we have a scheme that 'meets the program' and can be built in stages so that our Board of Trustees will have choices as to how much we would need to commit at the outset. I stress this because there is great interest among the board and other supporters of the museum in how our plans are progressing and I am

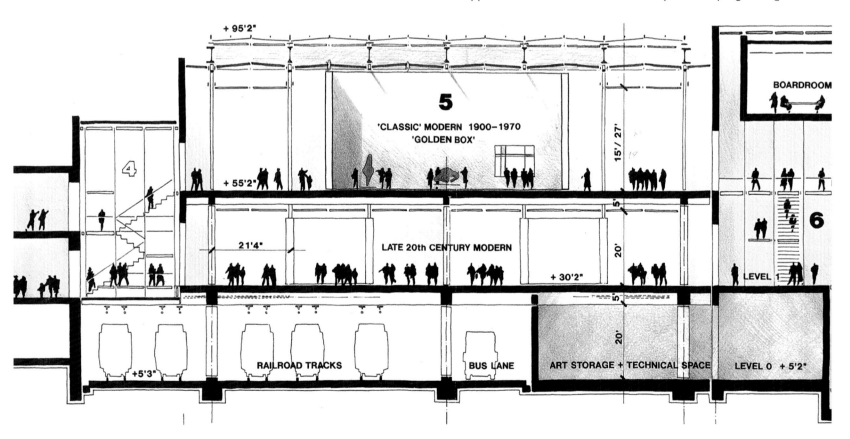

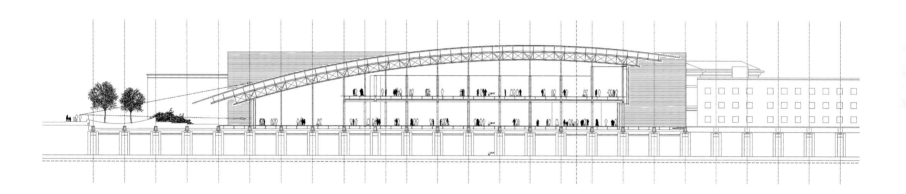

very eager to be able to share, at least an initial concept, with the Chairman of the Board and a select group of potential donors as soon as possible."[14] And he asked, although it was not "my primary concern at this point," whether or not the Columbus Drive entry could be given more consideration with regard to the pedestrian access to the new parking garage across Monroe Street to the north.

During the next workshop, in October 1999, the RPBW presented a scheme that could be executed in phases, building first south and then later north of Gunsaulus Hall. The curving roof could be phased similarly, allowing for dramatic north façades in the first phase, looking out over Millennium Park and the city beyond (figs. 11–14). Eventually, Piano held out hope that, when the two phases were complete, the "Golden Box" could be built on the second floor at the east–west axis connecting the south and north buildings. The RPBW also proposed a "theoretical" masterplan that modified the earlier one by SOM and found twice as much room for development on the Art Institute's campus (827,000 square feet instead of 400,000). At the same time, Wood had to report to the museum's Buildings and Grounds Committee that there were limitations and difficulties erecting a south building over the railway tracks. And he emphasized that any building would take into account the entire Art Institute site, that plans for this first structure would be done with the understanding that future buildings would no doubt be added at a later time.

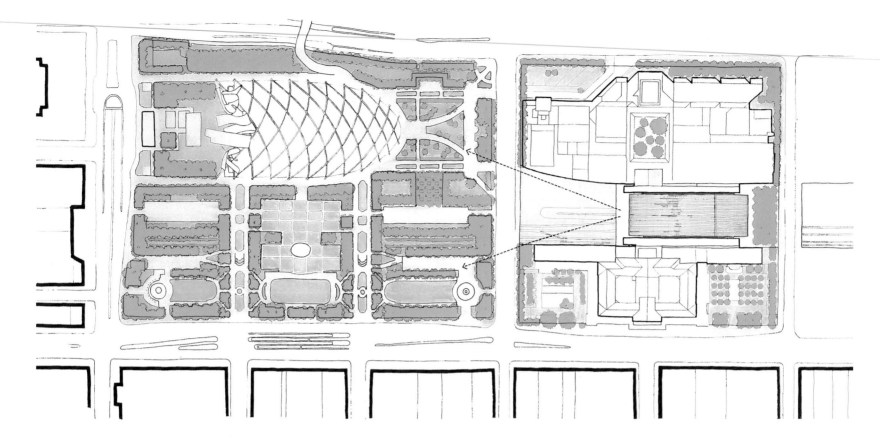

figure 14
RPBW, site plan of the Art Institute with a proposed addition over the railroad tracks, showing potential views toward Millennium Park, December 1999.

At the next workshop, two months later, the RPBW refined and simplified the previous design, distributing the building's program differently over three floors:

> First floor: Sculpture deck attached to Gunsaulus Hall on the north side and visible through north-viewing windows along the axial circulation spine in the renovated lower Gunsaulus Hall; galleries of contemporary art south of Gunsaulus Hall; and galleries of Himalayan, Indian, and Southeast Asian further south, overlooking a garden deck adjacent to Jackson Street
>
> Second floor: Galleries of "classic" modern art overlooking the sculpture deck to the north; a vestige of the "Golden" or "Magic Box" at the center point of the building's crossing the railway tracks
>
> Third floor: Woman's Board room on top of the east circulation tower with views east and north[15]

African and Pre-Columbian art were now assigned to future renovated galleries on the first floor of the Morton Wing, and galleries for ancient Mediterranean arts were no longer considered part of this project.

By March 2000 the schematic design was complete. Over the course of twelve months since the Art Institute had hired the Renzo Piano Building Workshop, eight design workshops had been held, during which engineering studies were considered and the design refined. The result was a scheme based on the following findings and principles:

> 1. The first floor of Gunsaulus Hall, through which 90% of the museum's visitors pass from galleries on the west side of the tracks to those on the east side, especially to the Regenstein Hall galleries where the museum's popular special exhibitions are shown, is a dark and low "tunnel" and should be replaced by "a clear and generous central 'street' which will create a central focus for the whole museum from which people can radiate to different galleries." It

should have views out to the north to bring light into the space and to orient the visitor. Its second floor should be "sacred" with a special place for "contemplation and enjoying art." This would require the demolition of Gunsaulus Hall. The implication of this approach is that the project's intervention into the museum's architecture was more "backbone surgery" than "plastic surgery."

2. Connecting the two floors of the New South Building to the existing floor levels of the Michigan Avenue Building did not allow for using the maximum possible square footage in the available air space over the railway tracks.

3. The main objective of the roof design is to provide quality natural light into the galleries. The roof construction consists of a 5-layered system: an outer sunshade made of laminated-glass tubes screened on one side with a opaque film to allow only 40% of daylight to filter through; a waterproofing and insulation layer made of a double-glazing system; a moveable-louver system to regulate excessive light; a laminated-glazing system to form a buffer space to prevent down-draft in the severe Chicago climate; and a translucent velum ceiling. The total roof package would be ten feet deep.

4. The exterior materials should be limited to stone, steel, and glass. The glazed gallery façades are made of a large-pane, double-façade system with slender steel wind bracing. Large custom-made translucent blinds will be necessary to avoid glare. The glass tubes for the outer layer of the roof will be gradually spaced out from each other toward the roof edge to give the roof a dematerialized character.

5. The character of the galleries should be restrained, similar to the museum's existing ones. For the second-floor modern art galleries, this means wooden floors and off-white plaster walls; while for the first-floor contemporary art galleries, this means a more industrial or loftlike finish: treated concrete floors and bare, smooth, finished concrete ceilings. All glazed elements should be made of "extra white" glass to avoid a green glow. And indirect lighting should be introduced in the artificially lit spaces and galleries to improve the perception of the spaces.

6. From a functional and architectural perspective, the Columbus Drive entrance is unsatisfactory. An inviting, large, transparent canopy oriented north and east could be introduced to connect to the proposed tunnel link from the Millennium Park Garage. And the east entrance itself should be clarified to enhance circulation at that point, and acoustics, lighting, and general architectural quality should be improved.

7. Along the perimeter, gardens should be introduced with a dense planting of trees to unify the various building volumes and integrate with a new, handsome, and permanent fence system, which is required by the crowds attracted to the area by the various summer festivals.

8. The roofscape of the northeast quadrant, including the derelict, former Goodman Theatre facility and the eccentric Rubloff Auditorium, needs to be refined and improved. Equally, the interior of Rubloff Auditorium should be renovated.

9. Finally, the Grand Staircase of the Michigan Avenue Building needs to be carefully reviewed, for in its current condition its massiveness prohibits views through it, east and west, along the focus line of the central street. A lighter-detailed staircase would much improve these conditions, although it is recognized that this is a controversial proposal.[16]

The final substantive alteration in the design, shortly before the schematic design was presented, was the substitution of a "layered system of horizontal glazed roofs" that Piano thought would "blend in more with the Art Institute's complexity of different roof shapes" than the earlier curved design (figs. 15–16).[17]

Among the more important challenges facing the project throughout its development were the railway tracks. It had always been recognized that building over them would be complicated, just as any project constructed in the air rights over another's property is more

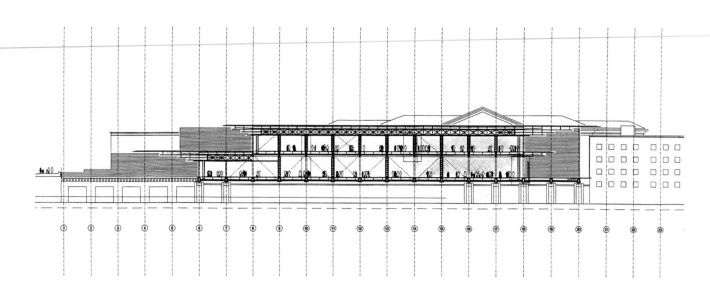

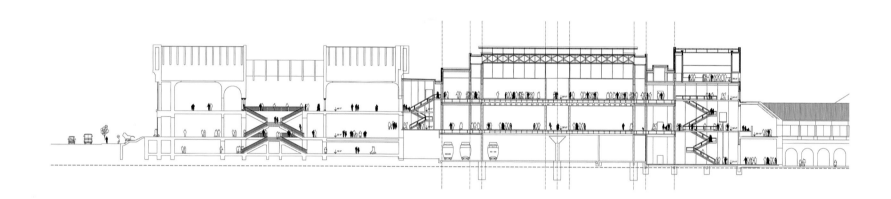

constraining and more expensive than building on a clean site. After lengthy discussions with the engineers from Ove Arup and Partners—the firm that collaborates with Piano on a majority of his projects—it was determined that the New South Building would require the construction of a 100,000-square-foot platform of considerable technical complexity at not insignificant expense. Furthermore, negotiations with officials from Metra (the regional railway authority) regarding the difficult logistics of erecting such a massive deck over their very active rail lines—and then lowering it into position—were far from settled. The railroad had lived with Gunsaulus Hall since 1916, but the prospect of accommodating new, *permanent* pilings set in place between its tracks to support a building and garden platform almost a city block long and of fixing the necessary clearance height in perpetuity, these matters were not winning swift approval.

After nearly fourteen months of such study, the AIC working group and the RPBW team decided to abandon the original plan and turn their attention instead to the site of the former Goodman Theatre on the northeast corner of the museum's campus. Obviously this was not an easy decision. More than a year had been spent considering the museum's needs in relation to the first site and refining and estimating the cost of meeting them. A core team of museum administrators, architects, and engineers had met numerous times, considered various options, and argued their positions, pulling and tugging against differing views, only to find in the end that the proposed design for the New South Building was neither satisfactory nor justifiable for its expense, especially when compared to the potential of the new site.

It is difficult to overestimate the investment of emotions involved in developing and refining a design scheme. Every participant has a strong view as to the potential of the project. The architect sees the larger picture and cannot easily limit his concerns to just a part of it, even if that part is said to be (perhaps) a first phase. The director, on the other hand, must always maintain the balance between what is needed—or at times *desired*—and what is affordable, financially and politically. Ultimately, the director has to convince the Board of Trustees that the project justifies the risk to be undertaken in funding it: what once was discussed as 70,000 square feet and later revised to 75,000 square feet has now become 194,000 square feet and easily more than twice as expensive. Why had this happened? Because the more one learns about a project and a site, the more one understands what needs—indeed *ought*—to be done. With every iteration of the design, with every workshop meeting, the project gets larger and more expensive, as well as more desirable and convincing.

That is simply the nature of projects; it was certainly the case with this one, given its peculiar site: a museum distributed unequally on both sides of railway tracks and south of what was becoming Millennium Park, a dramatic civic building project that had to be taken into account. With every passing month it was becoming evident that the museum's center of gravity was shifting from the Michigan Avenue entrance—along an east-west axis to which more galleries were to have been attached on the south—to a north-south axis with the potential of new galleries on the north equal in size and effect to those in the Rice Building to the south. The symmetry of the Beaux-Arts design of the Michigan Avenue building, which had been lost over the years with every new addition to the museum's physical plant, could perhaps be restored, with the museum having equal programmatic weight east and west, north and south.

Three months before the Art Institute took this decision, Frank Gehry revealed his designs for the new music pavilion. The plan placed it directly on axis with the former Goodman Theatre site. Both the pavilion and the garden south of it would be built over an underground parking garage, and pedestrian passageways were designed to connect the garage with the northeast corner of the museum's campus at Monroe Street and Columbus Drive. The increasing complexity and expense of the Art Institute's original plan over the railway tracks south of Gunsaulus Hall, occurring almost simultaneously with the development of Millennium Park, essentially compelled the museum to consider its options on a new site.

It was also the case that in November 1999 John H. Bryan had succeeded John Nichols as chairman of the Art Institute's Board of Trustees at what proved to be a very critical juncture. As noted earlier, Bryan had been intimately involved with the development of Millennium Park since its inception. As early as September 1997, at a reception overlooking the site that would become the park, Mayor Daley had pulled Bryan aside and gesturing toward it, had said, "We should build a park there." Two months later, in accepting the Daniel H. Burnham Award from the Chicagoland Chamber of Commerce, Bryan put forward the idea that in the spirit of Burnham's big plans a century before, Chicago should build a monument to the coming millennium. Then in March 1998, the mayor asked Bryan to lead a private fund-raising campaign to build a park on top of the new parking garage that was to be constructed over the Illinois Central Railroad tracks.

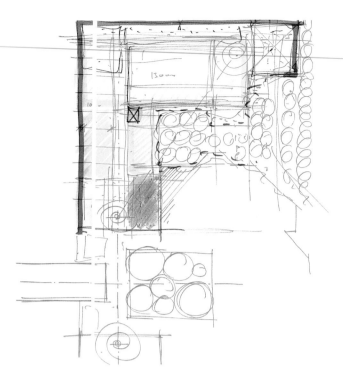

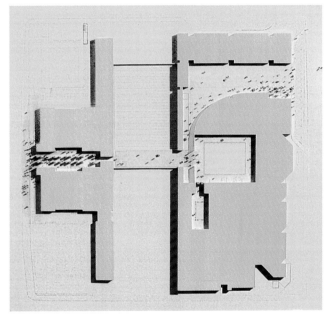

figure 17 (top)
Renzo Piano, conceptual sketch of a proposed addition to the Art Institute, North East Quadrant, June 2000.

figure 18
RPBW, model of a proposed addition to the Art Institute, North East Quadrant, September 2000.

Bryan was convinced that the park should include major works of contemporary art in keeping with Chicago's prominent earlier sculptures by Picasso, Chagall, Miro, Dubuffet, and Ellsworth Kelly. In pursuit of that goal he formed the Millennium Park Art Committee in July. Advised by the Art Institute's curator of modern art, Jeremy Strick, who drew up a list of possible artists, the committee settled on Jeff Koons and Anish Kapoor and asked each to propose a major, public sculpture. It also selected sites for the works: Koons's was intended for a terrace west of the pavilion's great lawn, and Kapoor's for the garden being developed along the lawn's southern edge just opposite the Art Institute's northeastern quadrant.

Around the same time, Bryan met with Cindy Pritzker and learned of her interest in having Gehry design the music pavilion. Once Gehry had accepted the commission, the role of the adjacent garden took on greater significance. Koons, whose 40-foot-tall topiary *Puppy* had recently been shown in front of Gehry's Guggenheim Museum in Bilbao, proposed for Chicago a 150-foot tower built of various materials, including children's toys, at the center of which was a publicly accessible water slide. The proposal met with opposition among key supporters of the park and Mayor Daley, and was rejected by the committee. Kapoor's proposal aroused greater enthusiasm, but its siting in the garden was seen as too confusing and the committee moved it to the site originally offered Koons (where Kapoor's *Cloud Gate* currently stands). That left the garden free of sculpture, and it was suddenly transformed in the eyes of Bryan and his committee into a destination itself, an organic counterpoint to Gehry's emerging tectonic, titanium-clad design.[18]

Eleven months later, in November 1999, Gehry presented his initial designs for the pavilion. The ambition was impressive, and for some on Bryan's committee, the recent relocation of the Kapoor and changes in the concept for the garden opened up "an avenue for dialogue" between the sculpture, the music pavilion, and the Art Institute. Given the emerging and seemingly irresolvable difficulties with its plans to build over the tracks, as described above, the museum increasingly felt the logical pull of the former Goodman Theatre site across the street from the proposed garden and on axis with the music pavilion. Having a Piano-designed building opposite the Gehry-designed pavilion with a destination garden in between was very attractive to many individuals involved in both the park project and the museum's expansion.

The Art Institute/RPBW team next met in June 2000. Under consideration was an initial schematic massing study for what was now referred to by all parties involved as the museum's "North East Quadrant." A four-floor, L-shaped building was proposed, with the long leg parallel to Monroe Street and the short one connecting with the Art Institute's McKinlock Court galleries. A garden was suggested for the space between the two legs of the L and the entire site was to be connected by a single basement. Entrance to the building was planned for the corner of Monroe and Columbus, to take advantage of the underground pedestrian tunnel that was to connect the museum with the parking garage beneath Millennium Park (fig.17). And for the first time, an education center was introduced into the program, increasing the project's size to 234,356 square feet.

At a workshop meeting a month later, a new schematic design was presented. The building would have five floors.

> Ground floor at track level: loading dock, art handling facilities, technical rooms, and art storage
> First floor: offices, architecture gallery, education center, sculpture court, gift shop, and an unspecified gallery, with visitor services amenities at the lobby entrance in the northeast corner

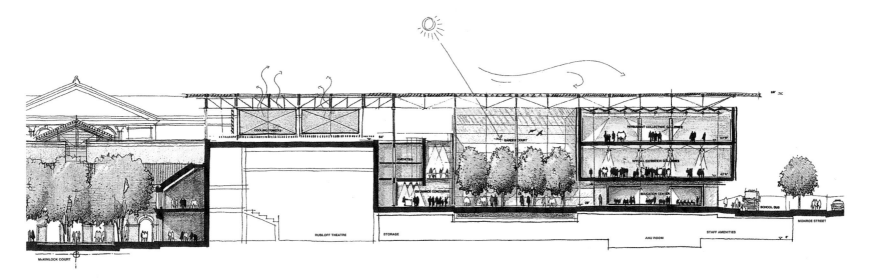

figure 19 (top)
RPBW, north-south section
of a proposed addition to the Art
Institute, North East Quadrant,
September 2000.

figure 20
RPBW, model of a proposed
addition to the Art Institute, North
East Quadrant, September 2000.

Second floor: 20,800 square feet of special-exhibition galleries, Architecture Department offices,
conference room, museum shop, and black box theater for multimedia presentations
Third floor: 30,000 square feet of permanent-collection galleries, café, and kitchen
Fourth floor: Meeting rooms and offices for the Board of Trustees and Woman's Board, and
a terrace[19]

It was also suggested that the new building would connect to McKinlock Court at two levels:
at the second level a walkway would tie into the second floor above Gunsaulus Hall and
ultimately the second floor of the Rice Building. Clearly, this new site for the addition was
inspiring a reconsideration of its program and its relationship to the museum's existing structures. The point remained that it was not only to add space to the Art Institute but also to improve
circulation within it. But the result thus far was hardly acceptable. As a first attempt to engage
the potential of the new site, it would change dramatically over each of the next workshops.

In September 2000 the team met to consider a new scheme, comprising just four floors.

Ground floor at track level: Loading dock, art handling and storage, technical services, offices, and
food services
First floor at street level: Museum Education center along Monroe Street (with a bus drop-off
on Monroe), garden court, sculpture garden, auditorium, retail shop, and north-south circulation
spine with an entrance on Monroe Street
Second floor: Special-exhibition galleries
Third floor: Permanent-collection galleries, café, art storage, and boardroom[20]

A major development at this stage was a proposal to move the main entrance of the new
structure back from the corner of Monroe Street and Columbus Drive to an addition to be
built onto the current Columbus Drive lobby. The pedestrian tunnel connection to Millennium
Park would be brought to this point for the convenience of visitors coming directly from the
parking garage. Others could enter from the street into an expanded lobby where they could
buy tickets and choose to go into the new building or the current building by way of McKinlock
Court, or could attend events in Rubloff Auditorium or dine in the museum's restaurant without entering the galleries. The irregular north façade of Rubloff would be regularized by a
curving wall forming a sculpture court north and west and enclosing a new, smaller auditorium
on the west, accessible from the main circulation spine (figs. 18–19). The guiding principle

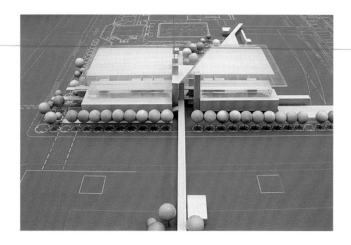

figure 21 (top)
RPBW, model of a proposed addition to the Art Institute, North East Quadrant, schematic design option 2, October 2000.

figure 22
Meeting at the offices of the Renzo Piano Building Workshop, Paris, January 2001, with, left to right around the table, Renzo Piano and Joost Moolhuijzen of the RPBW, Edward W. Horner and Rob Jones (partially hidden) of the Art Institute, Bob Lang (standing) of Ove Arup and Partners, Director and President of the Art Institute James N. Wood, Alexandra Nichols, life trustee Wesley M. Dixon, Jr., and trustee Andrew M. Rosenfield.

was not unlike that of the original scheme south of Gunsaulus Hall: a set of program spaces attached to one side of a circulation spine; in this case on the east rather than the south side. In total, the North East Quadrant building was now 249,790 square feet. All of this would be joined under a large, now flat, translucent roof of differing densities (denser over galleries than over gardens; fig. 20).

Only one month later, the scheme changed dramatically. The Columbus Drive entrance was abandoned and a new one was proposed on Monroe Street, halfway along the building. Underground pedestrian passageways from the parking garage would be extended from the Columbus Drive corner to this new point, from which two buildings would rise—a rectangular one to the east and a more or less triangular one to the west—with a new, diagonal circulation spine running between them to McKinlock Court and the intersection with Gunsaulus Hall (fig. 21). The front of these two buildings along Monroe Street would emphasize the education center to the east and retail shops to the west. The ground floor of the west building would also contain education classrooms and a sculpture court off the circulation spine. The second floor would have permanent-collection galleries in each building and, along Monroe Street overlooking the park, galleries for the collections of the Architecture Department in the west building and a media theater and trustees' boardroom in the east building. The third floor would have additional permanent galleries in each building, a café with an adjacent terrace in the west building overlooking the park, and more boardrooms and a terrace in the east building.[21]

Moving the entrance was a matter of concern with some museum trustees, both because it was yet another dramatic change and because it would likely increase the cost of the project. Many understood that such a move would—as Piano had anticipated—ultimately require the addition of either a bridge spanning Monroe Street or a canopied walkway across it. The resolution to the debate over the inclusion of (and the costs for) such elements in the total project would not be forthcoming soon. In a letter to John Bryan written two years later, Piano explained that his design achieved the only fully convincing connection between Millennium Park and the museum, a connection that could only be secured by an explicit link from one to the other, whether a bridge or a canopy. Piano argued for a bridge: "With the entrance moved to the west we have a great advantage that the bridge connects at the right place, giving people a sense of arrival at both sides [of Monroe Street]. If we make the bridge at the right level, it will offer a wonderful perspective over the gardens and Gehry's structure. The bridge becomes a 'belvedere' where people come for the view and enjoy [the] stay." Wood's priorities remained unchanged; he would answer Piano, "In the end, my greatest concern is that we do not allow the question of bridge-canopy-awning, . . . however it may finally be resolved, to become a tail that wags the entire building."[22]

The team next met in December 2000. The scheme had been refined but was more or less the same, except that on the second floor the boardroom and the terrace adjacent to it had moved to the west building, altering the footprint of the galleries from the previous, nearly square design to a long rectangle oriented north-south and opening gallery terraces on the north side of both buildings overlooking the park. Embedded south of the galleries were cooling towers, necessary for the building's technical services. Yet the placement of these cooling towers was controversial with some trustees, who wanted them moved to open up that space for additional galleries. It was suggested that they be relocated to the roof. Piano strongly disagreed. He argued for the purity of the building's geometry and the strength of the horizontal roof element in completing the building's form. The conversations about the

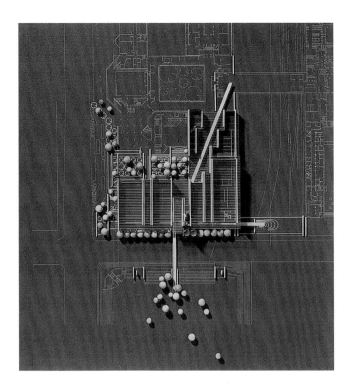

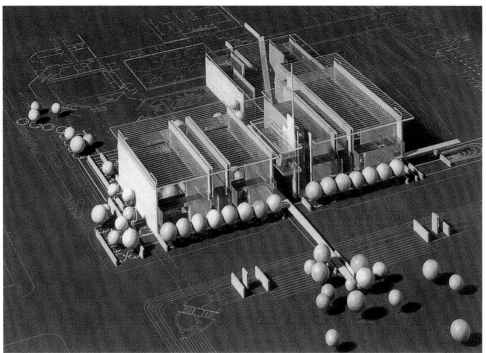

figures 23–24
RPBW, model of proposed addition to the Art Institute, North East Quadrant, January 2001.

cooling towers would continue for two years, until they were finally moved, at significant expense, south of Gunsaulus Hall to a site alongside the railway tracks where they were once to have been located in earlier schemes.

A January 2001 trip was arranged for key trustees to accompany Wood and the Art Institute team to a meeting in Paris with the Renzo Piano Building Workshop, expressly intended to build greater familiarity with and support for the project among those who would ultimately determine its fate (fig. 22). They were already convinced about the new program for the building, the new, northern entrance, and the clarity of "main street" (the circulation spine that would connect the building with McKinlock Court and thus with the Rice Building to the south). And though they were also pleased with the way the building had developed a dynamic, new relationship with Millennium Park, Wood wanted them to get even more familiar with and excited about the project. At this workshop meeting, Piano presented a further refinement of the current schematic design (figs. 23–24). The two buildings had become more regular in massing: two rectangular volumes with north-facing façades of more or less equal proportion on either side of the public entrance, marked both by the arrival of a bridge from Millennium Park at the second-floor level and a fourth-floor viewing platform and café topped by a dramatic, abstract, mastlike accent (fig. 25). The diagonal axis from the entrance lobby back to McKinlock Court was on two levels: through a sequence of sculpture courts and galleries on the ground floor and along a suspended walkway on the second floor (the walkway intersecting with an east-west terrace crossing between the two buildings). In plan, the new addition was square, incorporating Rubloff Auditorium and the museum's Columbus Drive entrance, from which through a new lobby (a remnant of an earlier scheme) one could cross through outdoor gardens to the new building (fig. 26). (Looking back on the strategic success of this session, and anticipating an important follow-up meeting in Chicago on April 26, Wood would later write to Piano on February 7 expressing his desire that the renderings that were being prepared emphasize the beauty of the views out of the building onto Chicago—views that he believed were comparable in quality to ones that the group had enjoyed overlooking Paris during their dinner in January at the restaurant on the top floor of the Pompidou Center.)[23]

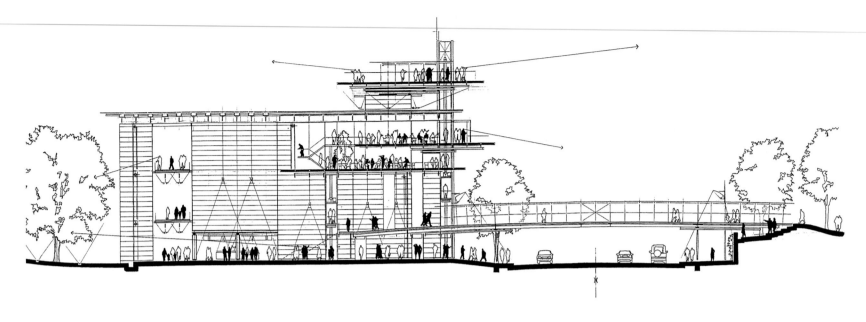

figure 25
RPBW, north-south section
of a proposed addition to
the Art Institute, North East
Quadrant, schematic design
option 2, April 2001, showing
4th-floor viewing platform
and bridge over Monroe Street.

figure 26 (opposite page)
RPBW, first-floor plan of
a proposed addition to the
Art Institute, North East
Quadrant, schematic design
option 2, January 2001.

Clearly the building was becoming more rational, as was its program: it positioned the education center, public amenities, and sculpture courts on the ground floor (what Piano liked calling the "profane level"); permanent-collection galleries on the second and third floors (the "sacred levels"); and a café on the fourth floor. A subsequent workshop hardly modified the design. And it was this scheme that Piano presented to the Art Institute's full Board of Trustees on April 26, and that the Art Institute introduced to the public in a press release on April 29, 2001.

When presenting this latest design to the board, Piano and Wood emphasized that the new building would engage with Millennium Park and with the Gehry-designed music pavilion; that garden spaces would "be prolific, both inside and outside the building" (a net increase of some 40,000 square feet of gardens) on the Art Institute site; that the building would demonstrate a commitment to energy efficiency, "meet our responsibility to the local community in terms of education, with facilities which will be unmatched by any other art museum," and strengthen the museum's "identity as a destination and as one of the major museums in the world"; and that it would "creatively resolve today's greatest challenge to the art museum, including the contradictions between contemplation and socializing, between education and relaxation, between art and commerce, and between the 'sacred' and the 'profane.'"[24] Also discussed were the ways the new building would affect the current buildings and distribution of galleries:

Galleries on the first floor of the Morton Wing would be dedicated to Asian art.

Galleries on second floor of the Morton Wing would be dedicated to medieval art, including tapestries and arms and armor.

Galleries for African and Pre-Columbian art would move to the second floor of Gunsaulus Hall, the first floor of which would remain for the Department of European Decorative Arts, although its limestone cladding would be removed for glazing to bring light into the center of the museum experience.

Current African and Pre-Columbian galleries would be converted into galleries for the Department of Prints and Drawings.

Southeast Asian galleries would extend from the north side of McKinlock Court into the new building.[25]

And when asked how the new entrance on Monroe Street would affect visitor traffic into the museum, Wood replied that by 2006, 60% of the museum's visitors would likely enter through the Michigan Avenue entrance and 40% through the new entrance, but because of the new underground parking to the north the comparison might even become 50%/50%.

In announcing the new location for the museum's expansion, it was said simply that the site "is the most appropriate location for the new building because it will allow for integration, both aesthetically and practically, with the new Lakefront Millennium Gardens across Monroe Street." It was also mentioned that the building would open a new entrance on Monroe Street, be connected by tunnel to the new Grant Park garage and a pedestrian bridge to the park, and would "enable vastly improved access for school groups." And it acknowledged that the abandoned Goodman Theatre building would have to be demolished.[26]

Sensing concern and perhaps even opposition from architectural preservationists, Wood remarked, "We appreciate that people have wonderful memories of performances at Goodman Theatre, but members of the Goodman's professional staff, including Executive Director Roche Schulfer, made it clear that the current space has serious shortcomings as a functional theatre."[27] And the press release went on to note that a 1988 study conducted by Theatre Projects Consultants, Inc., had "outlined serious limitations in the use of the space as a working theatre" and that its continued presence on the site "would preclude the logical construction of a building that requires excavation for mechanical functions and service facilities, severely reducing the potential development of the site."[28] Finally, it was stated simply that "it is not possible to build an elegant and functional building that would incorporate the former Goodman Theatre space."[29]

Over the next six months, the design was further refined. The first floor would still have an education center in the east building, but now the west building would include only a retail shop, coat check, and public amenities, and an exterior garden between the building and

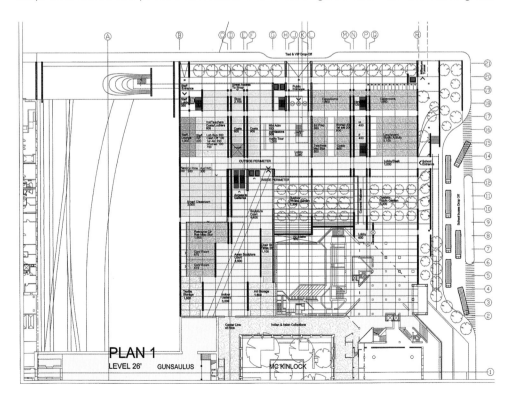

PLAN 1

LEVEL 26'   GUNSAULUS

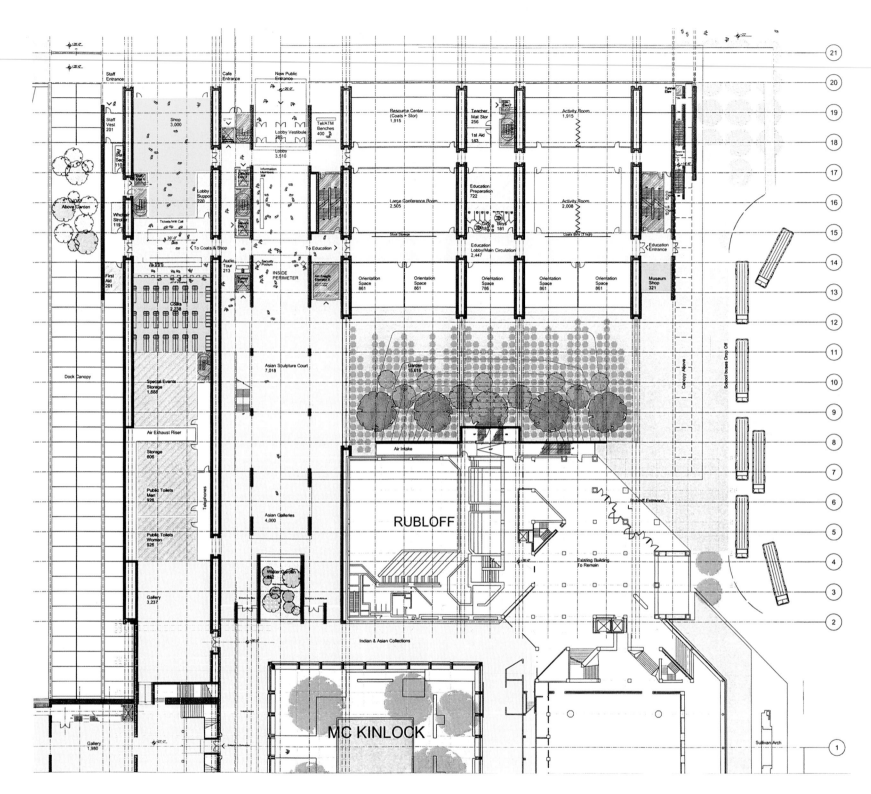

figure 27
RPBW, first-floor plan of a proposed addition to the Art Institute, North East Quadrant, schematic design option 2, December 2001.

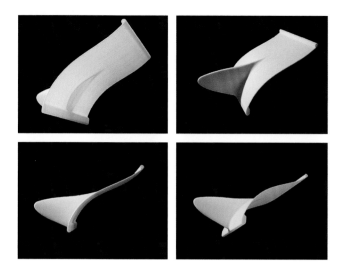

figure 28
RPBW, preliminary model for the design of the lamellas for the "flying carpet" sunscreen over the east pavilion of the proposed addition to the Art Institute, March 2002.

Rubloff Auditorium to the south. The central spine was now a sculpture court that could be converted into a generous social space for museum functions or catered events. The second floor comprised galleries for contemporary art in the east building and in the west building galleries for the Department of Architecture; galleries for small, temporary exhibitions of contemporary art; and ones for film and video. In addition, crosswalks between the buildings would be suspended over the foyer below, connecting on the west to a north-south walkway (Piano would come to call it a *passerelle*) that was an extension of the bridge to Millennium Park and ran the full length of the building to a gallery over a ground-floor winter garden at the point of connection with McKinlock Court. The third floor contained galleries for modern art in the east building and boardrooms in the west building, the two buildings connected again by crosswalks. And the fourth floor held only a restaurant in the west building, with a café terrace overlooking Millennium Park.[30]

Gallery ceiling treatments changed dramatically from vaults on both floors, open in the center on the upper floor, to a horizontal-beam structure on the second floor and a velum-panel ceiling on the third. The latter would gently diffuse the light that came through the exterior sunshade above glass skylights and into the galleries. The change in emphasis in the ceilings to verticals and horizontals (as opposed to round vaults) was in harmony with the vertical and horizontal structure of the buildings' exterior forms and interior organization. Ceiling heights in the galleries were fixed at 18'2" (16'9" clearance under the beams) for the display of contemporary art and 15'5" for modern art.

Importantly, the addition's entrance shifted further westward, on axis with the walkway in Millennium Park along the west edge of the garden, from the southwest corner of the Pritzker Pavilion great lawn to the western garage elevator pavilion (fig. 27). Piano knew this would be the "desire line" between the park and the Art Institute's building and thus to have an entrance anywhere but here was illogical. This necessarily reduced the width of the west building considerably from the previous design. It was now half that of the east building, which became the dominant building, not only in size but in presence too, for covering it was a large and dramatic sunshade Piano had begun calling the "flying carpet." This feature of the building—which would become a hallmark of the entire complex—had made its first appearance in April 2001. This carefully constructed sunscreen comprises rows of thin, curved plates, called lamellas, open northward to allow only north light to enter the building's skylights for the illumination of third-floor galleries, while the addition of fins perpendicular to the lamellas would help prevent eastern, southern, and western light from striking the skylights. Now made of extruded aluminum, these thin plates were originally to be fabricated out of laminated glass, and later fiberglass, and attached to a base framework comprising four structural "fractal" layers (fig. 28). In all, the "flying carpet" would be a square, 225 feet on a side, and include 4,800 individual lamellas, set at greater density over the building and lesser density over the garden, and be supported by twelve mastlike, tapered columns in the garden and four in front of the building, and by twenty-eight short masts (or "supports") over the building itself. The roof was basically to be a sunshade, but of course it was to be a grand, sculptural statement as well, capping the east building at the corner of Monroe Street and Columbus Drive with a powerful lateral element visible within the park and from great distances away. It was Piano's response to Gehry's ribbony, titanium forms of the Pritzker Pavilion. Piano would later remark that what Gehry's building did for sound, his addition to the Art Institute would do for light. Without question, while responding both to the program and the formal characteristics of the Art Institute's current buildings, Piano's design was also responding to the Pritzker Pavilion.

figures 29–30
RPBW, photograph of the existing Gunsaulus Hall building (top) presented in comparison to a photographic collage showing the renovation proposed for this wing of the Art Institute to expose its truss construction, September 2002.

In addition, the project continued to include significant modifications to Gunsaulus Hall. The hall's limestone exterior was to be removed and replaced by a glass curtain wall revealing the trusses of its bridge structure (figs. 29–30). On the lower floor, the north and south interior plaster walls were to be replaced with glass to allow natural light to enter those galleries (the residual "magic box" at the center of the Art Institute) and to offer views out onto the railway tracks and north to Millennium Park. It was not determined what collections, if any, would be displayed there.

In July 2002, the museum announced that the opening of its (at that point) $200 million addition had been pushed back to 2007 instead of 2005 or 2006 as previously assumed. Accordingly, the groundbreaking ceremonies that had been hoped for in January 2003 would now occur in either late 2003 or early 2004. The delays were principally necessary to enable the architects and engineers to resolve certain design complications related to the glass-walled exterior and the lower loading docks at the level of the railway tracks. "We are determined to put as much time into design development as necessary to solve all the challenges of this program to our and the architect's satisfaction," Wood was quoted as saying in an interview with the architecture critic of the *Chicago Tribune*.[31]

Nevertheless, despite the postponement, Wood said that fund-raising for the project "was off to a good start." He also noted that the addition might be smaller than previously reported—250,000 square feet rather than 290,000—and that the café intended for the upper level might be moved to the ground floor. At the same time, not reported in the press, the Art Institute and Piano were rethinking the bridge that would connect the addition to Millennium Park. In a letter to Wood, Piano's lead associate on the project, Joost Moolhuijzen, wrote that remarks that Wood and John Bryan had made regarding how the new entrance worked with the *passerelle*—which continued from the bridge through the building and connected to the two crosswalks between the east and west buildings—had made Piano think that the bridge might not work. "We have to admit that what we are asking pedestrians to do who come directly from Millennium Park is a bit tortuous. They have to climb a set of stairs, cross over Monroe, and descend on the other side. . . . Renzo's thought was to omit the passerelle and simply build a horizontal canopy right on the center line of the entrance and cross it over Monroe connecting to Millennium Park and the Pavilion, [and] install a set of traffic lights to allow people to cross safely." And he described the canopy as "a sharp, thin, and beautiful blade cutting the sky over Monroe."[32]

Two months later, in anticipation of a presentation on September 17 to the Board of Trustees that was intended as a status report on the project, and conscious of the financial impact that the 9/11 attacks on New York and Washington, D.C., had had on the country, Wood wrote to Piano acknowledging that the "biggest challenge facing the museum at this moment is the depressed American economy and falling stock market, and the very negative effect this has had on our ability to raise funds over the past twelve months." And thus, although they were pleased to have raised "nearly half of the $198,000,000 budget for the new building" [there was also the need to raise $87,000,000 in endowment for it], it has been decided that "it would not be responsible for the museum to proceed with working drawings until we have substantially more funding in hand."[33] The museum was thus forced to postpone the decision to proceed with working drawings for one year. An article in the *Chicago Sun-Times*, following the meeting of the Board of Trustees, noted that construction was now to begin in January 2004 with a completion target date of 2007. Wood was quoted as saying, "Our goal all along has been $200 million; the struggle has to been to retain that. But we're off to a good start. It's an interesting economy we're in. But we're optimistic."[34]

Piano replied to Wood's letter with one of his own expressing unhappiness that the decision to proceed with working drawings had been put off a year. "Is the building too expensive? I do not agree...Nothing is extravagant here. The Flying Carpet maybe? But the proportional cost of this strong, architectural, functional, and symbolic element to the overall scheme is only 5% or so."[35] Wood answered him on September 11, 2002—the first anniversary of the attacks—calling attention to the date and noting that his intention in his earlier letter had been "to be completely frank and honest with you about the very real difficulties that we have had raising money during this past year, the cursed anniversary of which falls on this very day." That said, he emphasized that the board's Executive Committee had a "firm and unanimous determination to realize this extraordinary building." And he discussed strategy regarding his and Piano's coming presentation to the full Board of Trustees.[36]

It was not the best of economic times. The Dow Jones was in the midst of falling from a high above 11,000 in mid-2001 to below 8000 a year later. While many economists argued that, after ten years of growth, the U.S. economy was firmly in recession, the Federal Reserve, in an effort to revitalize or at least stabilize the economy, cut interest rates ten times during the year. At the same time, the Art Institute learned that its endowment had dropped by $43 million when two Dallas-based hedge funds in which it had invested lost 90% of their value. In December the Art Institute filed a lawsuit against those responsible for these hedge funds; as Wood announced, "We are taking this action to safeguard all investments of the institute that are managed by these individuals and to determine exactly how the institute's assets were invested by them in the past." Word of this action spread quickly and articles appeared in both local newspapers and in the *Wall Street Journal*.[37]

Still, the Art Institute/RPBW team continued to work on the project, reviewing recent refinements to the scheme. At a December 18 meeting, a plan was proposed without a bridge and a sub-basement (the latter was dedicated to technical services which were reworked and included in the basement level at the loss of various offices and some storage space). In addition, the west building was reduced to include only two floors above ground: the first comprising a café, coat check, and a conference center; and the second, a boardroom, film and video gallery, and architecture galleries. (The space apportioned for these galleries was increased in size by moving the cooling towers southward to locations on either side of the east end of Gunsaulus Hall.) The education center on the ground floor of the east building was reduced by a third to include a retail shop. A bridge to Millennium Park was still being considered.[38]

Two months later, Wood wrote to Piano with good news: "The board has just voted unanimously to proceed. The racehorse has warm blood in its veins." The *Chicago Tribune* reported that "While some other museums are canceling expansion programs, the Art Institute of Chicago on Monday announced it is moving ahead with a new wing designed by the Italian architect Renzo Piano. Reflecting the weak economy, however, the portion of the wing devoted to galleries has been cut by 20 percent." It noted that the total square footage of the project had been reduced from 290,000 to 220,000 and that the portion dedicated to galleries had been reduced from 75,000 to 60,000. "Yes, the lady's a little slimmer," Wood was quoted as saying, but "I don't feel we lost any of its soul." The *Tribune* concluded by emphasizing the museum's announcement didn't mean that the museum formally committed to build the addition. "It only authorized the architect to complete blueprints over the next 12 to 14 months." The museum would decide whether to proceed only after contractors bid on the project as finally designed. (It also noted that the museum had raised $100 million against a building project goal of $198 million and an endowment goal of $87 million.)[39] It was also reported that the Art Institute had hired landscape architect Kathryn Gustafson, designer of the garden in Millennium Park opposite the museum's new site, to design the landscaping around the new addition and the proposed garden between the east building and Rubloff Auditorium.

The next seven months were dedicated to fund-raising and to resolving the matter of re-locating the cooling towers in order to maximize the square footage in the addition that was allocated to galleries. In anticipation of a workshop meeting in June, Wood wrote to Piano, "Hopefully, we can put the question of these bloody cooling towers to rest permanently and devote some time to the next level of design detail for the north elevation."[40] The cool-ing towers were finally relocated to a site south of Gunsaulus Hall, down at the level of the railway tracks.

With this decided, Wood wrote to Piano on September 8, 2003, to impart some news: "I will be making an important announcement to our Board of Trustees at tomorrow's Board meeting and wanted to convey its contents to you personally first. I have now been the director of the Art Institute for nearly 24 years and while there is no other museum job that I would prefer. . . I will be telling the Board that I intend to retire in the coming year once my replacement has been hired and is firmly on board." He concluded by affirming, "I can assure you that there will be no interruption in our working process and that I will be attending all of our meetings into the coming year and eventually look forward to introducing the new Director to both the underlying philosophy and mission as well as the details of the design solution for the new wing."[41]

Almost five full years after first meeting Piano and discussing with him the prospect of an ad-dition to the Art Institute, one that grew from 70,000 square feet to more than 260,000, and that moved from a site over the railway tracks south of Gunsaulus Hall to one at the corner of Monroe Street and Columbus Drive on axis with Millennium Park's Pritzker Pavilion; after various starts, stops, and restarts; and after numerous meetings with trustees and against the backdrop of 9/11 and the consequent downturn in the economy, Wood had the project on track: the Board of Trustees had approved the completion of construction drawings and the project's design was nearing completion. All that remained was to complete the design and construction drawings and have the board hire his replacement and give its approval to break ground on what was to be the largest addition to the Art Institute ever—a building the size of the museum's 1893 Michigan Avenue building and one, with its connection to Millennium Park, as important to the future of the museum and to the cultural center of the city as any ever undertaken.

In November 2003 Piano wrote to Wood pressing for confirmation on a May 21, 2004, start date for demolition: "You know my theory of fixing a target and making it: it's simple but it works." To meet this date, he acknowledged, the architectural team would have to produce a "demolition package" of drawings and schedules within two or three months and accelerate the production of construction drawings by one month.[42] Correspondingly, the Art Institute's fund-raising campaign would have to have reached $150 million (just over 50% of the goal). Neither of these was a small challenge. Raising funds for capital projects involves a kind of catch-22: trustees are reluctant to approve projects for construction until the majority of funds have been raised, and donors are reluctant to give to projects that have not been ap-proved for construction. At the same time, as long as a project remains in design development, or as long as construction drawings remain incomplete, design changes and refinements are

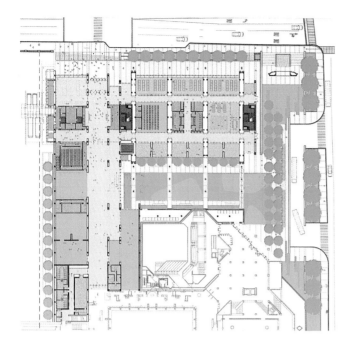

figure 31
RPBW, first-floor plan of a
proposed addition to the Art
Institute, North East Quadrant,
October 15, 2003.

likely to continue, often at a cost to the project. Without a commitment from the Art Institute's Board of Trustees to proceed with the project, fund-raising for the "New North Wing" was stalled and Piano continued to work on the design.

In November, he issued new plans strengthening the articulation of what everyone involved was now calling "main street": the north-south axis connecting the Monroe Street entrance with McKinlock Court (fig. 31). It now comprised a double-height, skylit arterial with galleries left and right. As one entered from McKinlock Court, the gallery immediately to the right was dedicated to South Asian sculpture, while that to the left was for small, changing exhibitions; further along to the left was one intended for Islamic art. Opposite the Islamic gallery was a large, two-story, glass curtain wall through which one could see, but not enter, the Kathryn Gustafson-designed garden. (Noting the importance of gardens in Islamic art, Wood wanted the museum visitor to connect the art on view in the Islamic gallery with the garden visible across "main street.") Now suspended in front of the glass curtain wall was an elegant stairway, providing vertical connection between the wing's first and second floors. At the north end were the information desks, coat check, ticketing counter, and gift shop, as well as the entrance to the education center.

This new clarity came with changes to the footprint and elevations of the building. The museum's recently constituted Building Oversight Committee expressed concern over these changes and their implications for the project's budget and schedule. In a letter to Piano, Jim Wood and Andrew Rosenfield, chair of this new committee, emphasized that while the committee approved the proposed changes, it was "greatly troubled by receiving such material (albeit useful) at this stage in the process." In addition, "[w]hile all agreed that these changes definitely improved both the function and aesthetics of the building, the Committee was deeply concerned that such design changes so late in the construction drawings process, if repeated, likely would jeopardize our ability to meet both the schedule and budget." They closed by saying they looked forward to meeting soon, hopefully before the end of January.[43]

It was at this time that I was hired to succeed Wood as president and director of the Art Institute. I had had a history with Piano, having worked with him from 1997 to 2002 on a renovation and expansion of the Harvard University Art Museums.[44] I left Harvard in January 2003 to direct the Courtauld Institute of Art in London, and a year later was invited to succeed Wood. I attended my first meeting on the New North Wing project in the Renzo Piano Building Workshop offices in Paris in June 2004. I assumed my duties at the Art Institute that September and shortly thereafter Piano came to Chicago for meetings.

Earlier that summer, Millennium Park had opened to the public. It was an instant success. Crowds played in the waters of the *Crown Fountain*, designed by the Spanish artist Jaume Plensa; laughed at their reflections in the polished surface of Anish Kapoor's *Cloud Gate*; lay on the lawn of the Jay Pritzker Pavilion; and walked through the Lurie Garden. Millennium Park is a cultural park, not a sylvan glade. Designed to attract and entertain thousands of people daily in the center of the city, it expands the public sphere—what was once private land far beneath is now public—and completes the development of Grant Park, connecting Michigan Avenue and Randolph Street with the lakefront in an integrated circuit of cultural, recreational, and commercial experiences. Almost overnight it became the new image of Chicago. As Frank Gehry pronounced at the opening, "What other city in America has a venue like this in its downtown?" And the public voted with its feet. Chicagoans and tourists alike came in the hundreds of thousands that first summer. Many of them no doubt looked south from the park directly to the loading dock of the Art Institute and the derelict and now empty buildings of the Goodman Theatre.[45]

During Piano's visit that October, he, John Bryan, and I—joined by trustee Thomas Pritzker, his wife, Margot, and his mother, Cindy—walked through the park. Piano hadn't seen it completed, and he was much impressed by Gehry's rambunctious pavilion and the sinuous bridge that crossed Columbus Drive. As we stared at the site of the New North Wing, it was obvious to all of us that we had to move ahead with this project. (Remember that Piano had hoped that we would have broken ground five months earlier.) It was also obvious that we had to connect the building with the park. And although we hadn't yet gotten permission from the Board of Trustees to break ground, nor raised the $150 million that the trustees wanted before proceeding, we encouraged Piano to revisit the idea of a bridge.

A month later we received Piano's first thoughts on the new additions to the project. A 600-foot-long bridge would rise from deep within Millennium Park, at the point where the east-west walkway between the *Crown Fountain* and *Cloud Gate* meets the great lawn of the Pritzker Pavilion, just opposite the entrance to the Gehry-designed bridge. It would connect to the west pavilion of the New North Wing at a new, third-floor level that would include a restaurant in the front, with views overlooking the park, and a sculpture terrace at the back (fig. 32). The idea was not at all what we expected, for we had thought that perhaps a bridge would simply cross Monroe Street to allow pedestrians safe passage from the park to the museum. We had not discussed connecting it to the museum or adding an entire floor on the west side of the building. These were not minimal changes, but they were brilliant. More than a pedestrian utility, the proposed bridge and the restaurant-and-terrace were a dramatic gesture linking the museum with the park and opening a second front door onto the newest cultural development in the city. Thus, it was with great excitement that we met in Paris in December to work through the newest plans.

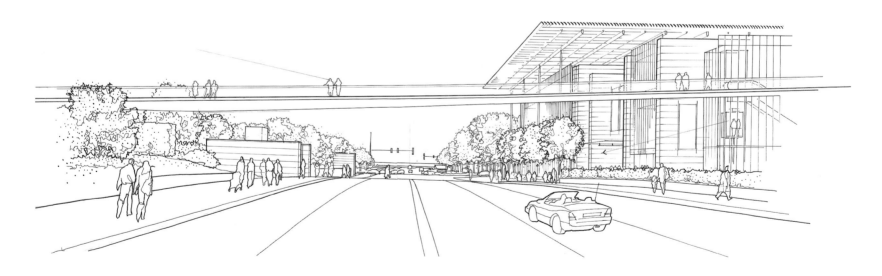

figure 32
RPBW, perspective rendering of the proposed design for a pedestrian bridge connecting the Art Institute's New North Wing addition with Millennium Park, December 2004.

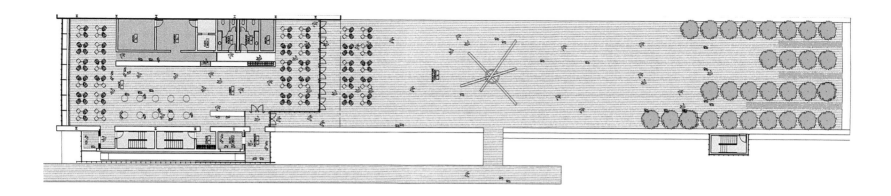

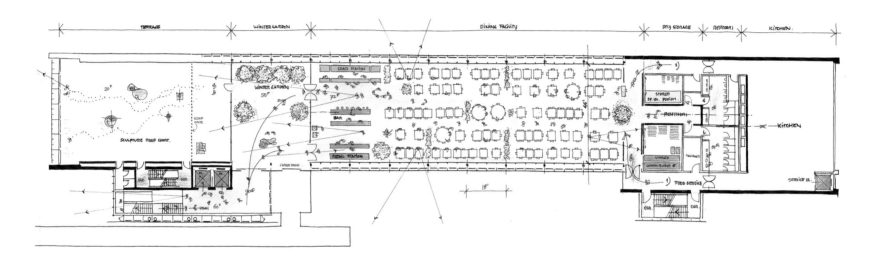

It was immediately obvious that the restaurant was in the wrong location. Piano had reason-
ably conceived of it as a venue from which to enjoy a view of the park, but this forced the
bridge (at greater expense) to extend farther south along the building. It also privileged
seating along the north-facing windows, dividing the restaurant between those who could
see the park and those who couldn't, and created a dead zone between the tables on the
north side and those on the south (fig. 33). By reversing the locations of the restaurant and
the sculpture terrace, we reduced the length (and expense) of the bridge, increased the
size and capacity of the restaurant (important programmatically as a venue for a variety of
museum events, and for third-party rentals), and allowed for more general, public access
to the terrace overlooking the park (fig. 34). This change meant that the public circuit from
Millennium Park led to the museum's free sculpture terrace rather than to the restaurant, a
decision that seemed much more in keeping with the social benefit of the pedestrian bridge
as the Art Institute's link with the park.

At the same time, we made changes to the program of the galleries off "main street." The
Indian gallery to the right was now given over to the display of works from the Department
of Photography, which had never been included in the plans for the wing, and the Islamic
gallery was converted into an extension of the temporary exhibition galleries. This clarified

the overall identity of the wing: it was now dedicated exclusively to our modern and contemporary collections of painting and sculpture, architecture and design, and photography and new media, film, and video, and to temporary exhibitions of the same. This had the effect, as we pondered the reinstallation of the galleries in our current buildings, of helping us realize that we could similarly clarify the program of each of our other buildings. That is, the Rice Building—save only the temporary exhibition space of Regenstein Hall—became a wing for American art. The second floor of the Allerton Building, extending into the second floor of the Morton Wing and across upper Gunsaulus Hall, was designated as a suite of galleries for the arts of Europe since the Middle Ages. The main floor of the Allerton Building, extending into lower Morton Wing, across the main floor of Gunsaulus Hall, and around McKinlock Court, would become a suite of galleries dedicated to the arts of Africa, Asia, and the Islamic world, as well as Indian art of the Americas and the arts of the ancient Mediterranean world. What had been previously a confusing sequence of galleries of unrelated cultures was now being reordered into four more or less coherent cultural experiences.

We met again in Paris in January 2005 and, among other things, considered the details of the bridge. It was to be curved at the bottom, like the shell of a racing scull, with glass banisters and wooden handrails, much like the suspended staircase within the building itself. The bridge would also be connected to the building by a three-story glass box within which would be an escalator and an elevator for visitors to descend into the building or rise to the rooftop sculpture terrace and restaurant. There was immediate concern about the utility of glass banisters for reasons of maintenance and the danger they might present to migrating birds. Of course, too, the shape of the bridge hadn't been reviewed by engineers, nor had its means of vertical support. Piano wanted it to have the fewest columns possible, so that it would appear to float: a gossamer thin blade rising effortlessly from the park at a 5.6% grade. By good fortune, the bridge could rise over the storage yard of the park and not take away a square meter of public space. This was important, because we hadn't yet received permission from the city to build a bridge across Monroe Street, let alone into the park. Given traditional opposition to structures that might disrupt views of the lake or occupy land in public parks, it was not at all certain that we could get permission to build the bridge.

A month earlier, however, John Bryan and I had met with Mayor Daley to discuss progress with the design of the building and to raise the question of the bridge. The mayor was still buoyant with the continuing positive local and national response to Millennium Park, particularly so since he had put his considerable credibility on the line championing it. The city had had a history of ambitious projects saddled with considerable cost overruns. The State of Illinois Building (now the James R. Thompson Center) from 1985, for example, was expected to cost between $75 million and $83 million, but ended up costing $173 million. Similarly, the expansions to McCormick Place in 1984–86 came in $60 million over the initial budget estimate of $252 million. During the design and development of Millennium Park, journalists were decrying its delays and increasing budgets (never mind that these were the result of changes that upon its opening in 2004 were much loved by the public and praised by the architectural press). But at various points in the process, journalists were describing it as "an expensive public-works debacle" characterized by "haphazard planning, design snafus and cronyism." The park's original cost estimate of $150 million rose to $370 million and finally $475 million. One critic called it "the biggest boondoggle of the Daley administration."[46] But now, seven months after opening, the park was the new symbol of the city: a public-private partnership gift to the people of the city, and a popular, cultural enhancement of the city's center and its famous park system.

The mayor was happy to talk about our project. He saw it as enriching Millennium Park as well as the Art Institute and further enhancing the development of the city's center. I had come prepared with books on Piano's work, including images of his Kansai Airport in Osaka, which is built on a man-made island connected to Osaka by a long, elegant bridge. My effort was unnecessary: Daley was very familiar with Piano's work (he had his own copies of the books I came to leave with him), and he was predisposed to like the bridge. In addition, he wanted to talk about the possibility of building a deck over the railway tracks just south of Monroe Street for the purpose of creating a sculpture garden adjacent to the site of the proposed new wing. Such a platform would effectively extend the park experience and further integrate the museum with the park. After all, he had just done the same thing with Millennium Park. Neither Bryan nor I was prepared for this proposal. It wasn't an idea that had been considered recently, nor, given the cost and difficulty of it, was it one that we wanted to consider at the moment. We were focused on the current project and needed Daley to concentrate on the bridge proposal. Fortunately, he did. We got his support, but only after we heard more about the benefits of burying the railway tracks beneath a sculpture garden. This may be a project likely to happen one day, such is the mayor's ambition. In the meantime, Piano continued to refine the bridge and its connection to the museum, as well as certain spaces within the new wing.

A black box gallery for film, video, and new media had been relocated from a second-floor gallery to the balcony over the south end of "main street," at the point of the second-floor connection to Gunsaulus Hall. This change had provided additional gallery space for contemporary art, but it compromised the experience of the balcony. It would also prohibit any future possibility of connecting to McKinlock Court at that level. While there is nothing at that level of the court now, the double height of the McKinlock Court galleries would allow for the construction someday of a second floor of additional museum galleries, connected equally to the second floor of the new wing and of Gunsaulus Hall. Anticipating this, we moved the black box gallery down to the first floor within galleries that had only recently been given over to the Department of Photography. Now adjacent galleries would present photography and new media, and the balcony was free to become a graceful introduction to the new wing upon entry from Gunsaulus Hall. It could also be a new social/retail space: a place for visitors to gather, have a cup of coffee or tea, and look out over the dramatic, skylit, double-height "main street."

But we had not yet gotten approval from the Board of Trustees to break ground on the project. We were hoping for a May 31 groundbreaking, the day after the Pritzker Prize would be given out in Millennium Park on the stage of the Pritzker Pavilion. We didn't want to miss the opportunity to capture the excitement of the Pritzker Prize, which of course had been given to Piano seven years before. But there was much discussion in meetings of the Executive Committee in February and March over whether we should delay the start of construction until we could integrate the bridge and the third-floor restaurant and sculpture terrace into the project's construction documents to get a single estimate and bid. Some Executive Committee members thought this more efficient and less expensive; others thought just the opposite: that delaying the project would cost more in general conditions by adding a year to the construction schedule. Ultimately it was decided to go forward in two stages: first with the base building and then as soon as possible with the bridge and third floor. It was also acknowledged that this would mean that the final construction cost of the entire project would not be known at groundbreaking, should we go ahead on May 31.

But to go forward we had to have sufficient funding in place. Precisely what that amount would be we didn't yet know. The project was now projected to cost $198 million, to which

we added a goal of $87 million for endowment, for a total campaign goal of $285 million. In April, Louis B. Susman, chairman of the capital campaign, announced that we had raised $162 million in cash and pledges. Two weeks later we reached $170 million. That sufficed: although it was less than fifty percent of our goal—for a building project whose cost was not yet fully determined—it was enough to get approval for a May 31 groundbreaking. It was the perfect date, one we had been focusing on for months. The previous day the world's architectural community would be gathering in Millennium Park, across from the museum's new site. And many of those who came would stay on and join in the festivities celebrating the start of construction on what would be not only the largest addition in the museum's history but the largest capital project of any cultural institution in the city in a century.

The groundbreaking itself was marked by speeches, confetti cannons, and music (fig. 35), and in the afternoon, a roundtable moderated by the television commentator Charlie Rose brought together Renzo Piano, Frank Gehry, and architectural critic Ada Louise Huxtable. The museum also opened that day a special exhibition of models and drawings of the New North Wing.[47] The announcement of the launch was well received by the press. A June 3 editorial in the *Chicago Tribune* praised the project. Daley was quoted as approving of the proposed bridge as "a 21st Century connection between the Art Institute and the city." The *Chicago Sun-Times* critic emphasized the "tale of temperaments" between Piano's design and Gehry's Pritzker Pavilion: the Art Institute's new wing is "a calm, quiet, subtle building, serenely unconcerned about matching the visual stopping power of its flamboyant neighbor to the north."[48]

We still had to raise more than $100 million and as yet had no naming gift, which we judged would be upward of $50 million.[49] The largest gift we had to date was not even close to that. It was a daunting task. No previous Art Institute capital campaign had totaled more than $60 million. Still, John Bryan, Louis Susman, and the campaign committee were not to be deterred.

Over the course of the next few months, we spoke to a number of people, and one family was particularly encouraging. Collectively they had already given very generously to the campaign; all of it anonymously, and that would remain their stance: they didn't want their name on the building. If they were to go forward with gifts reaching $50 million, they wanted the building to bear a title in keeping with the spirit of Chicago. Somewhere along the way it was John Bryan who suggested "the Modern Wing," conscious that this city was the "birthplace of modern architecture," a city that had rebuilt and redefined itself, that looked forward and anticipated changes in the economy and continued to grow in size and vibrancy, and that was also proud of its history as a city of immigrants, a city of new beginnings. In addition, the name fit the character of the building's architecture, which was quintessentially modern: of minimalist design, made of modern materials, sustainable in its efficient use of energy, and incorporating green technology. And of course, the collections it would house were modern and contemporary. Indeed, "modern" avoided possible confusion with the city's Museum of Contemporary Art. Thus, from so many points of view, "the Modern Wing" seemed just right. And it stuck. On December 16, a little more than six months after breaking ground on the project, we announced their gift. At the same time, we announced that we had increased our goal to $350 million, having raised more than $250 million already, with $80 million accrued in just the previous six months. The increase was caused by the addition of the bridge, the third-floor restaurant, and the adjacent sculpture terrace, all of which had been approved by the Board of Trustees in June. Still, we had to raise nearly an additional $100 million.

Most of the winter months were focused on completing construction drawings and finalizing details on the bridge, the third floor, and the connecting glass box. Piano wanted the bridge "to fly." He wanted it to be as light as possible and to have as little apparent structure as he could get away with. This was not easy. The bridge was to be 620 feet long and 15 feet wide, with a 198-foot span across Monroe Street at a height of 31 feet. On top of that, the famous Chicago winds required substantial structural and columnar support. In spite of the challenge, Piano pressed on. The shape of the bridge was modified, broader in profile to better distribute the load, and the glass banisters gave way to woven, stainless steel mesh: lighter, easier to maintain, and safer for migrating birds. Ultimately, Piano would eliminate the two exposed columns on the south end of the bridge. These would have been the tallest—and by far its most visible—supports. Instead, he elected to cantilever the bridge off the building so that it would appear to float, suspended alongside the building, to which it would be attached by a *passerelle*, or gangway, to continue the nautical metaphor of the bridge looking like an elegant shell of a racing scull.

In October 2006, trustee Kenneth Griffin and his wife, Anne, gave a large capital gift to the campaign, in recognition of which "main street" was renamed Griffin Court. Piano, however, remained unhappy with its design. He thought it was too heavy, too mural. On the first floor, for example, the west wall had only three small door openings in more than 200 feet. On the second level, it had only one door and a small window. This he changed by opening doors and windows on the first and second floors the width of the double-height curtain wall on the east side of the court. At the same time, doors in the east curtain wall were added to allow admission to the garden, which was now conceived to be experienced as a facility accessible from Griffin Court. Previously designed only to be seen, it was redesigned to be used by museum visitors. It would be fenced at the east end and simplified for greater use by visitors, who would be encouraged to refresh themselves by sitting in the garden in the shade of trees and the "flying carpet" sunshade. We discussed sculpture for the garden but decided not to complicate the use of the space, with one exception: we commissioned Ellsworth Kelly to make a fifty-four-foot-wide, white, fan-shaped sculpture for the south wall of the garden. It would be harmonious with Piano's architecture and an elegant whisper of an artistic statement; just right to claim the garden as an art museum garden, and no more (fig. 36).[50]

figure 36
Gustafson Guthrie Nichol, Ltd., preliminary perspective view of the proposed design for the Art Institute's east garden, March 11, 2008. Although the design of the garden was later modified and the use of vegetation on the north-facing wall was eliminated, the final product, now named the Tom and Margot Pritzker Garden, still features the commissioned work by American artist Ellsworth Kelly shown here.

At the same time, Piano was still working on the bridge—which had been approved by the Chicago Plan Commission in July 2006—refining its engineering, reducing its steel tonnage by forty percent, and simplifying its foundations. In November, Thomas Pritzker succeeded John Bryan as chairman of the board, the third chairman since the project began eight years earlier. The first, John Nichols, had stepped down from the board and had been succeeded as a trustee by his wife, Alexandra. Together they had given generously to the campaign, and in recognition of their generosity, enhanced by a recent, most extraordinary gift, we named the bridge in their honor. Over the course of the spring of 2007, as incremental improvements continued, bids for the bridge were received, and in June the trustees approved our going forward. Groundbreaking for the bridge was set for September.

We also began to revisit Piano's interest in Gunsaulus Hall. We had been presented a major gift from longtime trustee Marilynn Alsdorf, whose late husband, James, had been chairman of the Board of Trustees from 1975 to 1978. Their collection of Himalayan, South Asian, and Southeast Asian art, which had been the subject of a major exhibition at the Art Institute in 1997, included more than 350 works of art, many of them given or promised to the museum.[51] In many ways the scope and significance of the Alsdorf collection had prompted Jim Wood's interest in expanding the museum. As has been noted earlier, Wood initially thought that this collection would form the centerpiece of galleries devoted to South and Southeast Asian art on the first floor of a building over the tracks south of Gunsaulus Hall. In

figure 37
RPBW, winter garden in the
Menil Collection, Houston, 1987.

July 1999, following his appointment as architect of the project, Piano had proposed demolishing Gunsaulus Hall and constructing double-height galleries, principally to showcase the Alsdorf works in the new symbolic center of the museum. When Wood demurred, Piano responded by relocating the Alsdorf collection to galleries at the south end of the building that was to be elevated above the tracks, and providing these galleries with a prospect onto a garden deck. By 2000, once the museum had relocated its project to the former Goodman Theatre site, Piano kept his idea of displaying the Alsdorf collection in an open sculpture court adjacent to gardens, now in the North East Quadrant building (see figs. 26–27). In a 2003 design, the collection was given a discrete gallery adjacent to McKinlock Court with a view northward onto a garden (see fig. 31). When I arrived in September 2004, however, I displaced the Alsdorf works from this gallery, which I gave over to the Department of Photography (and to which we subsequently added a black box room for the display of new media, film, and video).

The decision to move photography into the new building was consistent with our emerging sense of the building's identity, but, at the same time, I remained displeased with Gunsaulus Hall. It was dark and windowless: tunnel-like. Filled with medieval and Renaissance European arms and armor and decorative arts, it oddly separated galleries of East Asian and South Asian art. The logical thing was to relocate the European arms and armor elsewhere (and they will now be shown together with medieval and Renaissance tapestries and sculpture on the second floor of the Morton Wing) and to present the Alsdorf collection in Gunsaulus Hall, where—almost five years earlier—Piano had originally envisioned it. But this would require considerable renovation. The first thought was to revisit Piano's 2002 plans to remove the exterior walls of Gunsaulus Hall, expose the railway truss structure, and glaze the hall's full length, north and south (see figs. 29–30). We briefly revived the idea of gardens on the north and south sides over the tracks; but these would have to be simpler gardens, more like the terrariums Piano designed for the African and Oceanic sculpture galleries in the Menil Collection, Houston (compare figs. 37 and 38). These would soften the light entering the gallery and provide a natural backdrop for viewing the sculpture.

Of course, we wouldn't carry this effect up through the second floor of Gunsaulus Hall because that area would contain painting galleries for our Impressionist and Post-Impressionist collection, and thus needed walls both for display and for the protection they provided from extreme natural light. Nonetheless, as we examined the possibility of demolishing the exterior walls, glazing the full length and height of Gunsaulus Hall on both sides, and rebuilding walled galleries on the second floor, we learned that that plan presented significant engineering complications: Gunsaulus Hall serves as the museum's umbilical cord and through its floors and walls pass essential electrical and communications lines, connecting systems on both sides of the museum's campus. With these complications came considerable, and ultimately prohibitive, expenses. More limited interventions—such as glazing only the north side, or glazing only part of the north side, or glazing only the first floor on the north side, or only part of only the first floor—all met with resistance from Piano. He had long envisioned opening up Gunsaulus Hall to light, thereby revealing "the truth" of its being a railway bridge. In the end, it was not simply a matter that we couldn't afford it; the fact was, we didn't want it. Yet we kept with the idea of opening up only part of the north wall on the first floor to bring light into the gallery, which would still enable us to exhibit and to protect light-sensitive works of art.

I wrote to Piano in December 2006 outlining the limits we wished to place on the Gunsaulus Hall project, specifically the main-floor galleries that were now to be named to honor the

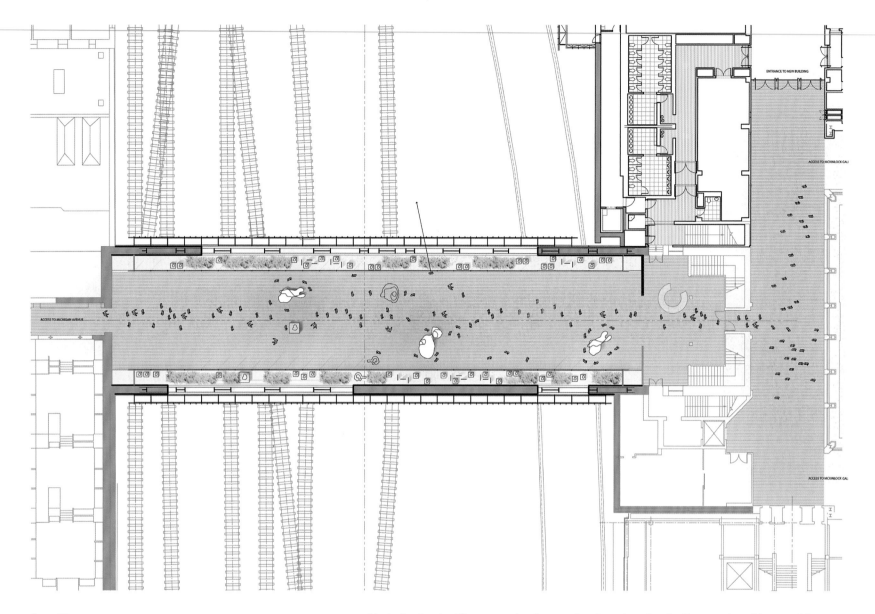

figure 38
RPBW, plan of the first floor of
Gunsaulus Hall showing the proposed addition of winter gardens
along the north and south walls
of the building, in conjunction with
the installation of the Alsdorf Galleries of Indian, Southeast Asian,
Himalayan, and Islamic Art. This
preliminary plan, dated November
16, 2005, was later altered.

figure 39 (opposite page, top)
View of downtown Chicago, looking
southwest, with the Art Institute
and the newly completed Modern
Wing and Nichols Bridgeway at
center, Millennium Park to the right,
and Grant Park visible at upper
and lower left, June 2009.

Alsdorfs. Again, Piano remained committed to the visual effect and architectural honesty of the 2002 proposal, or something quite like it. We, on the other hand, were increasingly concerned that any further delays in deciding the matter would preclude our opening these renovated galleries at the same time as the Modern Wing. Finally, by April 2007, we reached a compromise that respected our budget and still managed to bring a new design aesthetic to this space: the galleries were to be gutted on the main floor only and rebuilt with materials like those in the Modern Wing—white oak, plank flooring and white plaster walls and ceilings— with no interior walls and a fifty-four-foot stretch of windows open on the north side re- vealing the bridge truss. In a real way we had come back to Piano's earliest scheme for a light-filled, symbolic center of the museum. Sometimes over the course of a project as large and long as ours, earlier, abandoned ideas return and make all of the difference in the project's success.

Demolition began on the main floor of Gunsaulus Hall in November 2007, and the new Alsdorf Galleries of Indian, Southeast Asian, Himalayan, and Islamic Art opened in December 2008 (fig. 40). As we gathered on that occasion, we looked north from those galleries toward the Mod- ern Wing and the bridge to Millennium Park. Both were on track to open in May 2009, a full

figure 40
Installation of the Alsdorf Galleries of Indian, Southeast Asian, Himalayan, and Islamic Art in Gunsaulus Hall, December 2008.

ten years since Piano had been hired. When we began, the project was 70,000 square feet and was proposed to lie over the railroad tracks south of where we were standing. In mid-2000 the site was changed to its current one, just in front of us, and the size of the building was increased to over 234,000 square feet. It subsequently grew to 290,000 square feet, before shrinking back to 250,000 by the summer of 2002. At groundbreaking, four years later, it was 264,000 square feet, and there it has stayed (fig. 39). At the same time, the project cost had grown from $198 million at groundbreaking to $294 million at completion, with $87 million for endowment. In addition, we had undertaken $30 million of renovation and reinstallation of most of our earlier galleries, including the one in which we were standing. In all, as the product of imagination and ambition, of generosity and hard work, it had been an extraordinary decade in the life of this great institution, and with Millennium Park having opened halfway through this period, in the cultural life of this great city.

NOTES

1. The Art Institute of Chicago was founded in 1879 as the Chicago Academy of Fine Arts (and took its current name in 1882). It comprises equally a museum and a postsecondary school of art, each reporting separately to a common Board of Trustees. Its earliest properties, west of and then on Michigan Avenue, were temporary and quickly too small. In 1887 it constructed on Michigan Avenue at Van Buren Street a new building designed by Daniel H. Burnham and John Wellborn Root, but even this structure was soon outgrown. In 1890, Chicago's city and business leaders began planning the World's Columbian Exposition to be held in 1892 on the occasion of the 400th anniversary of Columbus's arrival in the New World. As with all such ventures, the Exposition was meant equally to promote its host city as a cultural center of international stature and to stimulate the city's growth and development. The earliest plans called for locating the Exposition in the city center in Lake Park (now Grant Park), but the cost of filling in the lake to expand the park to the required extent was prohibitive, and plans shifted to a dual site: mainly in Jackson Park on the city's South Side, with a limited program of activities scheduled for a new structure in Lake Park.

Although it was presumed that the Art Institute would take over the Fine Arts Building in Jackson Park after the Exposition closed, the Art Institute's trustees wanted the Lake Park site because of its central location. In December 1890, the Art Institute successfully negotiated for the rights to develop the lakefront with the Exposition's planners and to assume occupancy of the building on Michigan Avenue at the close of the fair. John Wellborn Root was once again called upon to prepare designs for the new building, but he died suddenly of pneumonia in January 1891 at the age of forty-one. The Boston-based firm of Shepley, Rutan and Coolidge—successors to the office established by H. H. Richardson—subsequently received the commission for the building for the World's Congress Auxiliary as the building was called (it was the Exposition's center for meetings, lectures, and exhibitions). It opened in 1893, and the Art Institute assumed the building in December of that year. See Linda S. Phipps, "The 1893 Art Institute Building and the 'Paris of America': Aspirations of Patrons and Architects in Late Nineteenth-Century Chicago," *The Art Institute of Chicago Museum Studies* 14, no. 1 (1988), pp. 28-45.

2. A Special Parks Commission had been established in 1899, and a 1904 report noted the paucity of city park land. Concern for the lack of free and open recreational space in the city contributed to the commissioning of the 1909 *Plan of Chicago* by the Commercial Club of Chicago. See Daniel H. Burnham and Edward H. Bennett, *Plan of Chicago,* edited by Charles Moore (Princeton Architectural Press, 1993), and Carl Smith, *The Plan of Chicago: Daniel Burnham and the Remaking of the American City* (University of Chicago Press, 2006).

3. See Lois Wille, *Forever Open, Clear and Free: The Historic Struggle for Chicago's Lakefront* (Henry Regnery, 1972), esp. pp. 71–81.

4. See Timothy J. Gilfoyle, *Millennium Park: Creating a Chicago Landmark* (University of Chicago Press, 2006), pp. 39–42, 63–76.

5. Key to the plan was the outdoor music pavilion. In anticipation of the Century of Progress International Exposition in 1933-34, the city erected a temporary band shell on the south end of Grant Park. From then until 1970, the free Grant Park concerts ranked among Chicago's most popular cultural events. Their success inspired park district officials to consider building a permanent lakefront music pavilion. An initial plan in 1936 proposed a sunken amphitheater in Butler Field, across Columbus Drive east of the Art Institute. A second proposal located the amphitheater at the southern end of the park. Further proposals returned the pavilion to Butler Field. Civic groups opposed the plan in part because they argued that it violated the Montgomery Ward rulings regarding built structures above grade in the park. An alternative was to replace the Monroe Street parking lot with a sunken parking garage topped by a recessed music pavilion structure. Other plans developed a site north of Randolph Street, returned to the Monroe Street parking lot site with a sunken band shell, and so on. None succeeded until Millennium Park. See Gilfoyle, *Millennium Park,* esp. pp. 21–77.

6. Twenty-three years after it opened, the Art Institute bridged the railway tracks that ran along its eastern edge with a two-story building (Gunsaulus Hall). Then in 1924 it added the Hutchinson Wing of galleries and the McKinlock garden court onto the east end of Gunsaulus Hall, and a year later the Goodman Theatre in its northeast quadrant. Additional wings for galleries were added to the Hutchinson Wing in 1927 and 1939, and, after a hiatus for World War II, an office wing was added to the Michigan Avenue building (B. F. Ferguson Memorial Building, 1958) and a gallery wing (Sterling Morton Wing, 1962). From 1974 to 1977, the Art Institute opened the Arthur Rubloff Building, a large project designed by Skidmore, Owings & Merrill, comprising facilities for the School of the Art Institute and a large auditorium, public amenities, and additional galleries for the museum, with a new entrance on Columbus Drive just south of the Goodman Theatre. Opened in 1988, the Daniel F. and Ada L. Rice Building, designed by the Chicago firm of Hammond, Beeby, and Babka, comprises gallery space for American arts, European decorative arts, and temporary exhibitions, as well as collections storage.

7. Established by the Art Institute in a building designed by Howard Van Doren Shaw and completed in 1925, the Goodman Theatre had become independent of the Art Institute in 1977, when the formation of the Chicago Theatre Group, Inc., meant that a new entity was thenceforth financially responsible for the Goodman's budget and personnel; see William Woodman and John Economos, "Report of the Goodman Theatre Center," *The Art Institute of Chicago Annual Report 1976–77* (Art Institute of Chicago, 1977), p. 22. In a separate agreement with DePaul University, effective July 1, 1978, the Art Institute ceded control over the Goodman School of Drama; see Rea Warg, "Report of the Goodman School of Drama," *The Art Institute of Chicago Annual Report 1977–78* (Art Institute of Chicago, 1978), p. 27. Over the course of the next two decades the Chicago Theatre Group grew increasingly dissatisfied with the limitations of its original building and began to search for a site in Chicago's theater district, a few blocks to the north and west of Grant Park, on which to construct a purpose-built modern facility. The Goodman Theatre abandoned its Art Institute site at the close of the 1999–2000 season, and opened in its new facilities in December 2000.

8. The SOM development analysis showed potential for constructing buildings and garden decks north and south of Gunsaulus Hall between Monroe and Jackson Streets and on the soon-to-be-vacated Goodman Theatre site at the corner of Monroe and Columbus Drive, connecting the museum by pedestrian underpasses to parking garages to be built by the city north along Monroe Street, and filling in various unbuilt spaces. In total, it found that 400,000 square feet of buildings and gardens could be added to the Art Institute's campus. The Art Institute plan was formally approved by the Chicago Plan Commission in May 1998. See Skidmore, Owings & Merrill, *The Art Institute of Chicago: Future Site Development and Master Plan* (Chicago, June 1996).

9. Renzo Piano to James N. Wood, Feb. 24, 1999.

10. See James N. Wood, "Report of the Director and President," *The Art Institute of Chicago Annual Report 1998-99* (Art Institute of Chicago, 1999), p. 4. Wood had first presented the SOM plan to the Art Institute's Buildings and Grounds Committee on September 25, 1998. At that time, it was agreed with the city, which had recently approved the AIC plan, that the Art Institute would provide additional open parkland surrounding the Art Institute, especially on its north and south sides. Wood noted that he was considering various options for building during the first phase of a much larger, long-term plan. And he showed how it was possible to build over the railway tracks south of Gunsaulus Hall, adding as much as 65,000 square feet, and north, adding perhaps as much as 90,000 square feet. He also noted that there was additional space in the Goodman Theatre area. But whatever the museum chose to do, he emphasized, would be undertaken in the context of its long-range plan and over the next several decades.

11. This was not without controversy. Yet the *Chicago Tribune* architecture critic expressed his disapproval of the opposition to the appointment of these non-Chicago-based architects: "Going out of town for architects isn't a sign of weakness. It is a symbol of strength, a way that great cities reinvigorate themselves, as well as the art with which we live." Blair Kamin, "Barrier Free. Outsiders, by Design, Should Be Adding to Chicago's Building Legacy," *Chicago Tribune* (Nov. 14, 1999). Jason Edward Kaufman noted it as well in the lead-up to his interview with Wood following the announcement of the selection of Piano. And Wood drew parallels between Piano and Gehry. When asked why Piano was chosen, he replied: "This is an architect who has a very strong sense of his own design identity, although he does not create a signature product . . . He's also an architect who—like Frank Gehry—really loves and responds to art, which obviously is terribly important when you're going to be designing a container for it." Jason Edward Kaufman, "A 75,000 square-foot Expansion Planned for the Chicago Art Institute," *Art Newspaper* (Sept. 1999), p. 20.

12. This summary has been condensed from Renzo Piano Building Workshop, *The Art Institute of Chicago, Workshop III,* July 1999.

13. James N. Wood, Notes, Workshop III, July 12, 1999.

14. James N. Wood to Renzo Piano, Sept. 16, 1999.

15. This summary has been condensed from Renzo Piano Building Workshop, *The Art Institute of Chicago, Workshop VI,* Dec. 1999.

16. This summary has been condensed from Renzo Piano Building Workshop, *The Art Institute of Chicago, New South Building, Schematic Design,* March 2000.

17. Ibid., p. 3.

18. See Gilfoyle, *Millennium Park,* pp. 97–122.

19. This summary has been condensed from Renzo Piano Building Workshop, *The Art Institute of Chicago, North East Quadrant, Workshop 2, Schematic Design Option 2,* July 2000.

20. This summary has been condensed from Renzo Piano Building Workshop, *The Art Institute of Chicago, North East Quadrant Building Project, Workshop 2.3, Schematic Design,* Sept. 2000.

21. See Renzo Piano Building Workshop, *The Art Institute of Chicago, North East Quadrant, Workshop 2.4, Schematic Design Option 2,* Oct. 2000.

22. Renzo Piano to John H. Bryan, Oct. 10, 2002, and James N. Wood to Renzo Piano, Oct. 18, 2002.

23. James N. Wood to Renzo Piano, Feb. 7, 2002.

24. Minutes from Special Meeting of the Board of Trustees, April 26, 2001.

25. Ibid.

26. Press release, "Art Institute Announces New Building Site," April 29, 2001.

27. Ibid.

28. Ibid.

29. Ibid. An article in the *Chicago Tribune* on the day the museum announced its plans noted, "There is likely to be an outcry from preservationists over the loss of the Goodman Theatre. But the executive director of the non-profit Landmarks Preservation Council of Illinois, which has placed the Goodman on its list of the state's 10 most endangered sites, acknowledges that the now-vacant theater may be hard to adapt to new uses. Severe functional limits, such as lack of room for stage equipment, forced the Goodman Theatre Company to move to a new North Loop home last year. Said the executive director, David Bahlman, 'I don't think we'll wage a campaign [to save the building] until after we see what Renzo's doing.'" A war was not waged and four years later, despite then being on Preservation Chicago's list of the "Seven Most Threatened Buildings," the Goodman was demolished. See Blair Kamin, "Art Institute to Stretch Out: Expansion to Raze Old Goodman Site," *Chicago Tribune* (April 29, 2001), sec. 1, pp. 1, 15.

30. See Renzo Piano Building Workshop, *The Art Institute of Chicago, North East Quadrant, Workshop WDD 2–4,* October 2001.

31. Blair Kamin, "Art Institute Slows Down its Timetable for Addition," *Chicago Tribune* (July 17, 2002), sec. 2, p. 2.

32. Joost Moolhuijzen to James N. Wood, June 14, 2002.

33. James N. Wood to Renzo Piano, Sept. 5, 2002.

34. Andrew Herrmann, "Art Institute Tweaks Its Expansion Plans," *Chicago Sun-Times* (Sept. 18, 2002), p. 5.

35. Renzo Piano to James N. Wood, Sept. 11, 2002.

36. James N. Wood to Renzo Piano, Sept. 11, 2002.

37. See Barbara Rose, "Museum Defends Investing Strategy," *Chicago Tribune* (Dec. 12, 2001), sec. 3, p. 1; Ianthe Jeanne Dugan, Thomas M. Burton, and Carrick Mollenkamp, "Art Institute Investments Lose Big," *Chicago Sun-Times* (Feb. 3, 2002), p. 14; and Ianthe Jeanne Dugan, Thomas M. Burton, and Carrick Mollenkamp, "Chicago Art Institute Learns Tough Lesson About Hedge Funds," *Wall Street Journal* (Feb. 1, 2002), p. 1.

38. See Renzo Piano Building Workshop, *The Art Institute of Chicago, December 18, 2002.*

39. See letter from James N. Wood to Renzo Piano, Feb. 10, 2003. See also Blair Kamin, "Art Institute Shrinks Plan for a New Wing," *Chicago Tribune* (Feb. 11, 2003).

40. James N. Wood to Renzo Piano, June 16, 2003.

41. James N. Wood to Renzo Piano, Sept. 8, 2003.

42. Renzo Piano to James N. Wood, Nov. 5, 2003.

43. James N. Wood and Andrew Rosenfield to Renzo Piano, Dec. 23, 2003.

44. The project was abandoned during my tenure for lack of endorsement by the Harvard Corporation, but it has since resumed under the leadership of the new director of the Harvard University Art Museums, Thomas Lentz.

45. Of course, despite its success with the public, Millennium Park was not without its critics. A *New York Times* writer called it "a sculpture garden on steroids," while a local journalist thought its crowded spaces were "as pleasant as any overcrowded city bar." There were also critics of the private-public partnership that built it. One called it a kind of "Logo Land" that was "built to generate buzz," noting the presence in the park of corporate naming rights and the prominent display of the names of the private and corporate patrons of the park's construction. See Gilfoyle, *Millennium Park,* pp. 341–56.

46. Ibid., p. 159.

47. See James Cuno and Martha Thorne, *Zero Gravity: The Art Institute, Renzo Piano, and Building for a New Century* (Art Institute of Chicago, 2005).

48. See "Flying Carpet Lands in Chicago," *Chicago Tribune* (June 3, 2005), p. 22; Blair Kamin, "Art Institute to Add New Wing," *Chicago Tribune* (May 31, 2005); and Kevin Nance, "A Talk with the Park," *Chicago Sun-Times* (May 31, 2005), pp. 46-47.

49. Progress on the campaign had been steady over the previous year, if slow. In January 2004, Louis Susman reported to the Executive Committee that we had raised $35 million. A month later, he reported that James Feldstein, our campaign consultant, proposed that we raise an additional $50 million before beginning construction and that this would take as much as another year. In May, Susman reported that we had raised $143 million, at which point the Executive Committee agreed that we needed an additional $50 million before sending the project out for bids. A month later, John Bryan noted that our goal was to have raised $150 million by October 2004. By September, we had raised $152 million. It was said that our goal was to break ground on the project in April 2005, but that this could always be delayed. A month later, we were still at $152 million. I argued that there was a lack of a sense of urgency among donors to commit at this time, since we still hadn't agreed to break ground on the project. It was decided that a formal decision should be made at the November meeting of the Executive Committee. The decision was taken on November 8, 2004, at which point we had raised $152 million against a goal of $285 million. In hindsight, the Board of Trustees took a chance on the project. We didn't know then of course that we would get our naming gift only a month later.

50. In December 2006, we made one other change. The building had been designed to have concrete floors in the contemporary galleries—a nod, as it were, to New York-style Soho loft space. But by now that seemed a cliché. It would be the only gallery floor that was not wood and should the galleries be used for other reasons in the future, it would be peculiar to have them concrete. So we changed them to the same white oak flooring of the other galleries.

51. See Pratapaditya Pal, *A Collecting Odyssey: Indian, Himalayan, and Southeast Asian Art from the James and Marilynn Alsdorf Collection* (Art Institute of Chicago, 1997).

THE MODERN WING A PORTFOLIO JUDITH TURNER

JUDITH
TURNER THE
AMBIGUITY
OF FLATNESS
JOSEPH
ROSA

JUDITH TURNER IS A NOTED American photographer whose subject matter is mostly architecture. Her signature style consists of highly abstract black-and-white compositions that play with the ambiguity of light, shadow, and tonality to heighten the aesthetic character of her subject matter and reveal visual relationships not readily apparent. Tonality is a very important aspect of her illuminating compositions. An example of this can be seen in the way she employs the sky—above or beyond an actual building—as a monochromatic surface that then becomes part of an overall composition, a planar component brought into the frame of the photograph. This methodology is furthered by a strong sense of light and shadow that allows elements of a building to be seen as abstract surfaces heightening its architectural essence without having the entire structure completely illustrated.

Turner's compositions reflect her training as a graphic designer.[1] Her aesthetic development also explains the ambiguity in the depth of her photographic work, which relates more to the flatness of an abstract two-dimensional construction than it does to the reality of her given subject. In addition, Turner worked professionally as a graphic designer, and in the mid-1970s started to explore the camera as another realm of artistic expression. One of her first architectural subjects was Peter Eisenman's House VI, photographed in 1976. It was through Eisenman that Turner was introduced into the world of architecture and started photographing some of its most significant buildings. Yet it was her first book, *Judith Turner Photographs Five Architects*—published in 1980—that truly solidified her reputation as the photographer of this emerging, avant-garde voice of architecture.[2] Turner's volume came out eight years after the seminal publication of *Five Architects: Eisenman, Graves, Gwathmey, Hejduk, Meier,* which contained critical essays and drawings along with an assortment of photographs by numerous individuals that left the visual record of these architects' built work the book's weakest aspect.[3] In sharp contrast, Turner's timeless black-and-white photography—and a selection of some color images—connoted the formalist qualities of these architects, furthered their aesthetic ideology, and defined each architect's personal idiom.

Turner's work operates outside the realm of commercial architectural photography and is visually more aligned with the art photography of Florence Henri and Alexander Rodchenko.[4] The American-born Henri was trained at the Bauhaus as a painter—not a photographer—and this background had a significant influence on her later work, as can be seen in her use of mirrored surfaces in photographs that fracture the figurative compositions and engage spaces beyond the framed image. Rodchenko, a leading figure of the Russian Constructivist movement, was also trained as an artist and worked in numerous media from painting and sculpture to graphic design and photography. Henri's and Rodchenko's education outside of the medium of photography allowed their later photographic works to be encoded with an aesthetic ideology that was foreign to that medium. Turner's training as a designer and not a photographer allowed her to understand visually an architect's intention and to reveal it in compositions that she constructs and edits through the viewfinder of her camera. Her photography can be seen as a metalanguage of architectural intention and as an artistic expression that is inseparable from the representation of this built work. This methodology is the foundation for all Turner's work—which now spans over three decades—and is essential to understanding her own ideology, which explores the ambiguity of flatness within these well-composed photographs.

Whether her subject matter is contemporary or historical in its origins, these timeless poetic framings communicate an aesthetic quality that is purely hers. An example of this can be seen in even a small selection of her earlier photographs.

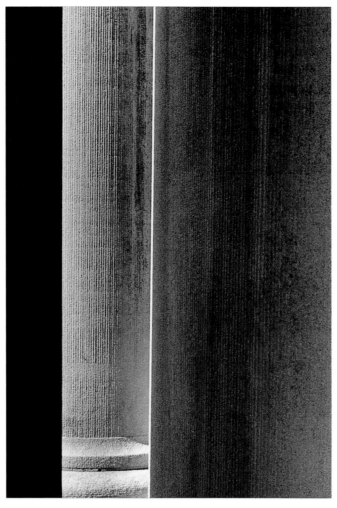

Turner's 1976 photograph of Eisenman's House VI, for example, is a study in tonality that captures a definitive detail exemplifying the architect's notion of an "absence of presence in architecture."[5] The simple framed view depicts a geometric condition at the junction of wall and ceiling where a void in the ceiling plane (and the floor above) is displaced into an adjacent space (fig. 1). Turner captures this gesture in an abstract image that visually reads as a composition of contrast and tonality, ranging from pale to dark. The framed view is further heightened by a strong diagonal—where the vertical wall and horizontal ceiling planes meet—that bifurcates the vertical composition, forcing the viewer's eye into the center of the image.

An example of how complex Turner's framings can be is seen in her 1979 series entitled *Columns.* In one vertical image (fig. 2) there are four bands of varying width and tone. To the left is the darkest one, while to the right of this is a portion of a Doric column that appears to have been collaged into the overall composition. This becomes apparent through the presence of a narrow vertical white strip that interrupts the base of the Doric column on its right side, separating it from the last vertical band of medium tonality. Collectively, this photograph reads as a study in tonal range and collage that renders the figurative quality of the columns ambiguous in relationship to the other vertical elements. This photograph is not a collage of disparate images, but instead one that depicts conditions found at the site. Two of the tonal bands are Doric columns from a colonnade and are in different degrees of shadow at one moment. The narrow white band is actually the glare of the sun shining on the adjacent right

column, which is in the immediate foreground of the composition. The simple position of this column in the foreground visually cuts off the base of the most legible column—the one that is most "in focus" and that is farthest from the camera.

A study in tonality and line can be seen with Turner's 1998 photograph of Hillside West in Tokyo by Fumihiko Maki (fig. 3). This horizontal composition is bifurcated by a strong diagonal that separates the frame from dark to light. This gradation, coupled with shadows from exterior balconies that are integrated into the overall composition, renders the depth of surface articulation ambiguous. In reality, the darker triangulated surface is one of the façades of the building, while the light horizontal lines are from the metalwork on the adjacent façade. Turner photographs the building's corner at a horizontal angle, conceptually flattening the building and visually allowing the two façades to read as one contiguous surface.

Turner's 1999 photograph of Smith-Miller + Hawkinson's Corning Glass Center is an example of ambiguity and clarity (fig. 4). In this vertical photograph the focus is on an assembly of metal elements that compose a railing for a parapet wall. The framing of this view, however, is mysterious and renders the collection of metal pieces ambiguous in its purpose and location. The photograph is taken from beneath a balcony and focuses upward, visually terminating on the vertical metal support of the railing. Turner's rendering of the underside of the balcony as a dark, monochromatic surface adds mystery to its location, while communicating the architectural aesthetic that is purely Smith-Miller + Hawkinson.

To commemorate the completion of Renzo Piano's Modern Wing for the Art Institute of Chicago, the museum commissioned Turner in 2008 to employ the building as a backdrop to her photographic lens. Piano's design is an elegant rectilinear building with beautiful details. Turner's photographic discoveries of the building reveal these attributes and their complex visual relationships—from the building's Cartesian structural grid, to its palette of materials, to its engagement with the sky beyond. These photographs help us further understand Piano's architectural ideology, and they provide us insights into the poetics of form and materials, the essential dialogue that is always a timeless condition in architecture.

An example of this can be seen in one of Turner's photographs that is a beautiful vertical study in the range of tonality and the ambiguity of flatness (see p. 70). Upon close examination one perceives the repetitive pattern of Renzo's horizontal "flying carpet"—bathed in light—that fills the left frame of the image. At the right side of this composition is a compressed view of the vertical window mullions that cast a gradation of shade and shadow onto the adjacent vertical limestone wall of the building. An important aspect of this photograph is the plane of the sky that fills the center portion of the image and becomes the third element in the composition. Turner has taken these three discrete aspects of the building—the horizontal, the vertical, and the sky beyond—and has visually collapsed them into one ambiguous figure-ground composition possessing a range on tonality from light to dark. It is simply that brilliance in seeing—beyond the actual building's normative character—that allows her to produce such timeless black-and-white compositions highlighting the underlying beauty of whatever it is she views.

Her ability to see, edit, and record—through the camera—allows us to witness the rich aesthetic qualities of Piano's Modern Wing. From its "flying carpet" to its walls of limestone with vast spans of glass, Piano's design for the Art Institute is a welcome addition to the lexicon of modern buildings in Chicago, and it provides as well a tranquil interior spatial experience that allows the art—and views out onto the city—to take center stage.

NOTES

This essay is based on interviews with Judith Turner conducted in the spring of 2009.

1. Turner received her degree in graphic design from the School of Fine Arts, Boston University.

2. See Judith Turner, *Judith Turner Photographs Five Architects* (Rizzoli, 1980). The book contains an introduction by John Hejduk. Other books by her are *White City: International Style Architecture in Israel* (Tel Aviv Museum, 1984); *Annotations on Ambiguity: Judith Turner Photographs* (Axis Publications, 1986); *Judith Turner: Tokio Marine Plaza Building, Osaka* (Kajima Design, 1991); *Tokio Marine Oyama Training Center, Photography by Judith Turner* (Kajima Design, 1994); and *Judith Turner: Near Sitings, Photographs 1975–1995* (City Arts Center, Oklahoma City, 1995). See also *Between Spaces: Smith-Miller + Hawkinson Architecture, Judith Turner Photography* (Princeton Architectural Press, 2000).

3. This volume was published in New York in 1972 by Wittenborn in response to a 1969 meeting by the Conference of Architects for the Study of the Environment (CASE) at the Museum of Modern Art.

4. For more on Florence Henri, see Diana C. du Pont, *Florence Henri: Artist-Photographer of the Avant-Garde* (San Francisco Museum of Modern Art, 1990) and Jean-Michel Foray, *Florence Henri* (Electa, 1995). For more on Alexander Rodchenko, see Christina Lodder, *Russian Constructivism* (Yale University Press, 1983) and Selim O. Khan-Magomedov, *Rodchenko: The Complete Work* (MIT Press, 1987).

5. For more on Peter Eisenman, see *Eisenman Inside Out: Selected Writings 1963–1988*, edited by Mark Rakatansky (Yale University Press, 2004).

RENZO PIANO
MODERNISM, MUSEUMS, AND THE TRADITIONS OF CHICAGO
PAUL GOLDBERGER

EVERY BUILDING IS A NARRATIVE, but Renzo Piano's design for the Modern Wing of the Art Institute of Chicago is really three of them, and they are inseparably intertwined: the story of Piano's architecture, the story of Chicago, and the story of the Art Institute itself. It is tempting to think of this building as a kind of manifest destiny, a saga in which one of the most eminent architects in the world at last gets the chance to build in America's first city of architecture when he receives the commission to expand one of the world's great museums. That is, in fact, what happened, and if it were necessary to describe this project in a sentence, it could do. But to leave it at that would be to miss what Piano himself would consider essential, which is the depth of the connection between the three strands of this story: the way in which this building is the product of Piano's previous work, particularly his other museums; and how it is also his attempt to respond to the traditions of Chicago architecture, which as an Italian he not only knew but romanticized more than many American architects did; and finally how it is his solution to the complicated programmatic needs of the Art Institute, which before Piano came onto the scene was housed in a complex of disparate buildings that, whatever their appeal, could never be described as coherent. Piano has managed to create a building that is at once consistent with his own architectural vocabulary, deeply resonant to the architectural history of Chicago, and responsive to the needs, both functional and aesthetic, of the Art Institute. And he has also designed in the Modern Wing a work of architecture that is highly responsive to its physical surroundings: it fits into the context of Chicago not only conceptually, but literally.

The new wing—serene, white, pristine, light—would seem, at first glance, to have little in common with Piano's first major building, the Centre Georges Pompidou in Paris, designed with Richard Rogers and completed in 1977. The Pompidou is intense and loud, an urban adventure in high-tech that to the Paris of thirty years ago seemed a cartoon as much as a serious building (fig. 1). It was a determined, not to say assertive, Modernist intervention into the heart of a city that, for all its connections to the avant-garde, had allowed almost no modern architecture into its center. But the Pompidou was softer and more warmhearted than it pretended to be, and you could see in it all the things that would come to define Piano's work as his career moved forward: a love of the sheer fact of construction, and a desire to express how a building is put together; a fondness for intense color, always played off against white, gray, or some other neutral tone; a determination to express human scale, and to make it clear that, however large and flamboyant a building might be, it would never become a wholly abstract object; and a sense of texture and of fineness of detail and craft— not always easy to see at the Pompidou, to be sure, but present in its way, awaiting the refinement that other commissions would make possible.

Those other commissions would come not to Piano and Rogers, whose partnership was limited to the Pompidou Center, but to Piano's own firm, established in the mid-1960s as Renzo Piano Architect and since 1981 called Renzo Piano Building Workshop, as if to underscore his interest in the nuts and bolts of construction. Piano is the son of a contractor, and he has lived his entire life around buildings and the act of making them. His hobby is sailing, and he has designed several sailboats. To him the essence of architecture is in the tectonic reality of a building; however sympathetic Piano is to an architecture of intellectual substance, theory is never what drives his designs. Yet he is unusually reflective for such a determinedly nonacademic architect, particularly one whose buildings are so clearly responses to circumstance, to both structural realities and the realities of program and context. Piano loves to talk, and he is exceptionally articulate on the subject of his buildings, even in English, not his first language. The appeal of Piano's conversation about his work is that

figure 1 (top)
Renzo Piano and Richard Rogers,
Centre Georges Pompidou,
Paris, 1977.

figure 2
Renzo Piano Building Workshop,
interior "promenade" in the Menil
Collection, Houston, 1987.

it is conversation, not pontification. He appears to be thinking aloud, and even if he has said something a hundred times before, he presents it as if it were a thought just beginning to develop.

When Piano describes a museum as "a secular meditation, a place of calm silence," you feel as if you are present at the gestation of his ideas. When he calls the museum "a soft machine for art" (a reference to the Art Institute of Chicago, though it sounds more like the Pompidou), it does not seem to contradict the idea of the museum as a place of reflection, because it is in Piano's nature to think of buildings as complex, and to recognize that they often need to possess many qualities at once. For Piano, the very essence of the challenge of an art museum is to make it a soft, flexible machine and a place of meditation, at once. If he did one of these things or the other but not both, he would consider himself to have failed. And when he says that "architecture is about passion, but it is also about time, and when you find yourself with something that works it takes patience, and then you find something that feels inevitable," he is able to make you feel a sense of the deep, slow process of search more than the triumph of discovery. You understand that the discovery comes only after the patience of careful search.

In Piano's case, the circumstances of every building project inevitably dictate the starting point. But they barely hint at a finishing point—that is key. You might say that Piano's architecture is the product of circumstances filtered through his calm, deliberate, and precise aesthetic sensibility. Ultimately his intuitive design instincts shape his architecture. His buildings vary tremendously from one to the next, but the absence of an easily identifiable style hardly means that there are not strong and clear formal ideas that join all of his work together and make it unmistakeably his. The firm's name may contain the words "building workshop," but Piano's own name precedes it.

If most of the particulars of Piano's aesthetic sensibility were evident in some form or another in the Pompidou Center, it would evolve considerably as Piano moved forward with work on his own. What the Pompidou was best known for, beyond its sheer brashness, was the open, loftlike space of its interiors, which Piano and Rogers had assumed would be reshaped for each exhibition. It did not always work as planned, and eventually the space was redesigned with more permanent partitions, but even here, there is at least some connection to Piano's later museums, which tend toward large exhibition spaces. There are almost never conventional rooms in a Renzo Piano museum. In the Menil Collection in Houston (completed in 1987), his first American commission and the project that firmly established him as a major presence among museum architects, there is a series of galleries that open in sequence to a wide, open promenade (fig. 2). The scale is far more modest than at the Pompidou Center, almost domestic in fact, but the sense is still of open, flowing space.

When Dominique de Menil, a patron and collector of extraordinary acuity, hired Piano in 1981, she was responding not so much to the Pompidou as a work of architecture—its exaggeration of Modernist detail to the point of parody was not her way of doing things—as to her sense that Piano had the potential to be an aesthetic heir to Louis Kahn, whom she had first hired to design her museum, a commission cut short by Kahn's death. (Piano worked briefly for Kahn in the late 1960s, before the Menil commission was received.) The Menil, a 402-foot-long, two-story-high box of steel, wood, and glass, is so understated that it could almost be taken for an American Modernist beach house blown up to civic scale. Yet it turns out to be a knowing and subtle melding of postwar American Modernism, contemporary

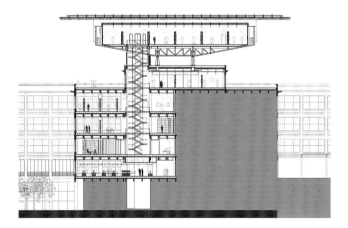

technology, and traditional American small-town urbanism, all put superbly to the service of a demanding and sensitive museum program. Piano's roof is the remarkable thing here, a complex structure of curved louvers that control both light and ventilation within the galleries below. The louvers, dubbed "leaves," are held in place by white iron trusses above, and the roof extends out beyond the galleries themselves to become, in effect, the primary visual element of the exterior.

The Menil has a sense of lightness that Kahn's buildings do not. But it shares Kahn's embrace of natural light and his desire to temper and control it by means of some kind of architectural device that could be lyrical on its own, as well as Kahn's ability to combine disparate materials into a serene, self-assured, gracious, and restrained whole. The Menil has the same aura of a Kahn museum, the same sense that light and materials are combining to create space that feels transcendent, almost sacred. But Piano renders this through structure that feels light and tensile, almost nimble.

The most direct descendant of the Menil came several years later, in Switzerland, when Piano was called to design a museum outside of Basel for another knowing collector, the dealer Ernst Beyeler. The Beyeler Foundation Museum, completed in 1997, is larger, and its exterior is a combination of reddish stone and glass rather than the clapboard and glass of Houston, but the roof structure owes a clear debt to the Menil, and is even more markedly a monumental architectural element on its own (fig. 3). Not long after that came Piano's Giovanni and Marella Agnelli Art Gallery, added in 2002 to the old Fiat factory at Lingotto, in Turin, Italy. Piano had been converting the factory to cultural uses since the 1980s, and the gallery, built onto the roof of the former factory, was the final phase of a long, adaptive reuse campaign. It is a tiny museum, a jewel box of metal and glass, set so as to appear almost to float on the roof. Atop it is an oversize louvered canopy, spreading out beyond the four sides of the building to give the small museum a monumental presence: a roof atop the roof (fig. 4).

Piano used a somewhat different roof structure in Dallas, at the Nasher Sculpture Center, completed in 2003, but again the idea was to make the roof a light, tensile structure that confers a sense of dignity and grandeur on more modestly scaled gallery spaces below it. In the case of Nasher, Piano created low, gentle barrel vaults of glass, set between parallel walls of stone (fig. 5). The glass is suspended atop narrow steel ribs and supported by thin steel rods anchoring it from above.

Not long after that, in 2005, Piano finished in Atlanta an expansion of the High Museum of Art, the first in a long sequence of American museum projects that, unlike the Menil, involved existing institutions that wished to expand and had been having difficulties either with their existing buildings, or with previous expansion schemes, or both. In the case of the High, a Richard Meier building from the mid-1980s that was admired more as a Modernist object than as an environment for the display of art, the need was for additional exhibition, public, and administrative space that had to manage the delicate balance of being simultaneously compatible with the Meier building and a corrective for it. Piano devised a scheme consisting of three pavilions, each of which was sheathed in panels of white-painted enamel similar in appearance to Meier's porcelain-clad steel panels (fig. 6). But where Meier's building is assertively sculptural, Piano's pavilions are simple in shape—carefully positioned boxes that together form a new entry piazza, appearing to defer to Meier's original wing while at the same time taking control of the sequence of public arrival and departure.

figure 5
RPBW, gallery within the
Nasher Sculpture Center,
Dallas, 2003.

figure 6
RPBW, entrance façade of
the Susan and John Wieland
Pavilion of the High Museum,
Atlanta, 2005.

at a time of immense technological change. At a time when old ways of construction were falling by the wayside, Chicago had to build fast and in great quantity, and it had no choice but to embrace the cutting edge. It is no surprise that the steel frame found its clearest early expression in Chicago, not in New York; although New York would become better known for skyscrapers of great height, Chicago was where the towers that most clearly expressed the idea of structure arose. Both cities, in their way, were pragmatic, but Chicago's pragmatism was based in a belief in clarity and structural logic, and it led directly to the creation of critical architectural ideas that formed the basis for what was to become known as the Chicago School. New York's pragmatism, by contrast, was the pragmatism of commerce, a constant push to make things bigger and cheaper. Instead of supporting the city's highest architectural intentions, it seemed at odds with them, a force for compromising ideals rather than for realizing them.

Piano has spoken eloquently of the role of Chicago in his own development as an architect. "The mythology of Chicago and the invention of steel construction loomed large in the imagination of people living on the other side of the Atlantic," he has said. And Piano, as an architect who has always freely admitted, even celebrated, his roots in the nature of construction—he is most likely to talk of Pier Luigi Nervi and Jean Prouvé when the speaks of his European influences, for example—understandably feels a link to the culture of what by any measure is America's most tectonic city. He delights, for example, in talking about the Chicago window, a common feature of early Chicago skyscrapers which consisted of a large fixed center pane of glass flanked by two smaller sash windows, which represents a nearly perfect blend of elegant form and practical function, demonstrating not only that the steel frame can yield a wide expanse of glass but also that it can be the basis for an appealing aesthetic.

Relatively few architects from abroad have built in Chicago in the last generation—Josef Paul Kleihues of Berlin, whose Museum of Contemporary Art opened in 1996, and Tadao Ando, who designed a house for a private client on the North Side, are rare exceptions—but Piano is probably the one most suited to the city, since his philosophy of architecture, if you can call it that, has so much in common with the Chicago tradition, not just in its formative years at the end of the nineteenth century and the beginning of the twentieth, but also in its continuation in the work of Ludwig Mies van der Rohe; Skidmore, Owings & Merrill; and others in the post-World War II years. Piano likes to reveal structure; he likes to build in glass and steel; he likes to make functions clear, and he likes most of all to create beautiful forms that, however much they may express structure, are also pure compositions, essays in mass and balance and solid and void. At its best, Chicago has always tried to do the same.

Piano also understands, as the Chicago architects did, that as a product simultaneously of technology and of culture, neither of which is static, architecture must always be evolving. Thus he recoils from historical replication, as the architects of the Chicago School always have. And like them, he neither disdains beauty nor has illusions that its achievement in architecture can be disconnected from everything else that a building needs to be.

"Architecture is very pragmatic, but in the end it is pragmatic because you are looking for emotion," Piano has said. "You want the wall, and you want the light, so how do you get these things? How do you make them happen? It is about detail and refinement. You can be both powerful and refined. As an architect you have to be both a poet and a bloody builder."

The central wing of the Art Institute of Chicago on South Michigan Avenue, whose façade established the institution's architectural identity more than a century ago, was not designed

by a Chicago architect. Neither does it have anything to do with the Chicago School of architecture. It is a proper Beaux-Arts building by the proper Boston firm of Shepley, Rutan and Coolidge, who erected it as part of an entirely different event in the city's architectural history, the World's Columbian Exposition of 1893—Chicago's famous "White City." The Exposition, overseen by the Chicago architect Daniel H. Burnham, launched the City Beautiful movement in the United States, making grandly scaled, classical buildings fashionable as civic monuments. City Beautiful was a countervailing force to Chicago's Modernist tide, and it would ultimately have at least as great an impact on the nation's cities as anything William LeBaron Jenney, John Wellborn Root, Louis H. Sullivan, Charles B. Atwood, or any of the other early Chicago Modernists would produce. Perhaps it should be considered no surprise that Sullivan would write that the 1893 Exposition was "a virus" that would set American architecture back "a half century, if not longer."

The Art Institute, through its Burnham Library, is a prime repository of archives relating to the Chicago School, and over the years, the institution has paid extensive homage to the legacy of Chicago Modernism through numerous exhibitions and works of scholarship. But so far as its own architecture is concerned, the Art Institute's attitude has been nothing if not ambivalent. A limestone box, the B. F. Ferguson Memorial Building, was added by the architects Holabird and Root and Burgee in 1958, its starkness a concession of sorts to Modernism, but it seemed more like a suburban government building than a civic monument, and it possessed neither the aspirations to grandeur of the original Beaux-Arts building nor the crisp elegance of good Modernism (fig. 8). The Sterling Morton Wing by Shaw, Metz and Associates, four years later, made a similar statement of blandness, and while this portion did not compete with the original Shepley, Rutan & Coolidge building, neither did it engage it in any kind of meaningful dialogue.

In the years that these wings were going up, Ludwig Mies van der Rohe was Chicago's preeminent architect. He was invited to design museums in Houston and Berlin, but the museum of his home city appeared to show no interest in offering him, or any of Chicago's leading architects, a commission. The museum did finally turn to Walter Netsch of Skidmore, Owings & Merrill in the early 1970s to expand the complex east of the Illinois Central Railroad tracks. Netsch, whose masonry buildings relied heavily on diagonal geometries, produced a sprawling set of stone-clad wings, later named the Arthur Rubloff Building, that only compounded the banality of the earlier additions, were awkwardly related to the older buildings, and were internally confusing besides. Set inside the building is the main trading floor of Louis Sullivan's Chicago Stock Exchange, rescued and reconstructed in the museum by the architects Vinci-Kenny in 1977. It is a splendid restoration, but you cannot avoid the sense that Sullivan's interior masterpiece has been all but buried, with the 1970s wings of the Art Institute a less than sympathetic sarcophagus.

In the 1980s, responding to the rising tide of interest in historicist architecture—or perhaps despairing of ever commissioning a significant modern building as a part of its campus—the Art Institute asked the Chicago architect Thomas Beeby of Hammond, Beeby and Babka to design a more frankly classical wing to be added to the south of the SOM sections. The Daniel F. and Ada L. Rice Building, as the Beeby section was called, turned out to be more refined and subtle, in its way, than the original Michigan Avenue wing, and it was unquestionably the best thing the Art Institute built in the twentieth century. But in light of the uneven record of the other phases of expansion, the success of the Rice Building sent an odd message for a Chicago institution of the visual arts, which was that to do well at the Art Institute, an architect would be advised to stay away from designing anything that hewed too close to the Chicago School and the Modernist traditions that were so vital a part of the city's cultural history. It was as if Chicago's architectural legacy belonged on the Art Institute's walls (or inside them, in the case of the Sullivan room); it was not to shape those walls themselves.

Renzo Piano, obviously, felt no such inhibition. "Everything in the Art Institute is stone, and Chicago is a city of steel," he said. Piano's rapport with Chicago was both tangible and conceptual; he embraced the city's architectural legacy, and he came to the Art Institute not just willing but eager to design a building that would reveal the parallels between his own work and the traditions of the Chicago School. But if Piano's work has always had a kind of theoretical connection to the Chicago School, it has been equally responsive to context, and here Piano was faced with the irony of a Chicago commission whose context seemed un-Chicago-like, or at least at odds with Piano's vision of what Chicago stands for architecturally. His challenge, in a sense, was to design a building that would simultaneously respect the Chicago Modernism that he reveres, as well as the existing buildings of the Art Institute that had been designed with relatively little regard for that tradition.

That conflict of context—Piano's own work and the legacy of the Chicago School together forming one context, and the existing buildings of the Art Institute making for a very different one—might be said to sum up the stylistic challenge for Piano. The architect also had to deal with the unusual and complex internal organization of the Art Institute, which, because its large site is bisected by railroad tracks, requires that one section serve as a bridge, making the overall layout something like an hourglass: wide at the Michigan Avenue entrance of the original building, narrow in the middle across the tracks, and wide again for the Netsch- and Beeby-designed sections. Piano loved the tracks, in part for their very inappropriateness on the site of the museum. Late in the project, he redesigned Gunsaulus Hall, the narrow section of

the museum that bridges the tracks and that used to feel more like a tunnel than a bridge. Piano inserted windows so the tracks would be visible. "It is absurd, those tracks," Piano has said. "The poetry of the trains, Route 66, right through the middle of the museum, it is wonderful."

As Jim Cuno explains in his essay, after an earlier site had been explored, Piano's addition was designated for the northeast corner of the museum compound, north of the Skidmore, Owings & Merrill wing, at a location that has almost as much visibility as the original building, since it faces two wide streets, Monroe Street and Columbus Drive. More important, it places Piano's façade squarely across from the large and busy Millennium Park. The final site made it clear that the building Piano was asked to design would not, like most of the previous additions, be an attempt to slip a new structure discreetly into a large complex in the hope of assuring that the institution's identity would still be set by its original Beaux-Arts building. Piano had the opportunity at the Art Institute, as he had at the High Museum in Atlanta, the Morgan Library in New York, and the Gardner Museum in Boston, to create a façade that would give the institution a new public face, one that might even some day become its primary one.

If more people see the original façade of the Art Institute every day as they pass it on Michigan Avenue than will see Piano's new façade from Millennium Park, Piano's façade will probably get far more lingering gazes. It is sumptuously sited, with what may be the nation's most popular new urban park spread out before it, and—as a late addition to the program—the punctuation mark of a soaring pedestrian bridge designed by Piano to take visitors from the park across Monroe directly into the upper levels of the new Art Institute wing. The 620-foot-long Nichols Bridgeway complements another footbridge on the other side of Millennium Park designed by Frank Gehry, which makes this surely the only place in the world with a Piano bridge and a Gehry bridge as neighbors. Gehry also designed the centerpiece of Millennium Park, the Jay Pritzker Pavilion, and Piano organized the interiors to give several of the main galleries views of the band shell, turning Gehry's swooping metal shards into a de facto piece of sculpture in the Art Institute's collection.

The Art Institute's Modern Wing, as it is called, is dominated by a three-story section, roughly square in plan, that presents a façade to Monroe Street and Millennium Park that is ur Piano, a mix of glass and metal and stone that possesses the dignity and clarity of classicism, and the crisp, tensile energy of Modernism (fig. 9). The metal is white, the stone is a limestone similar to that used in previous wings, and there is more glass than any public section of the Art Institute has contained. The glass is detailed in a manner that gives new meaning to the

figure 10
Detail view of the glass curtain wall
of the Monroe Street façade of the
Modern Wing of the Art Institute,
February 2009.

term "curtain wall"—it is set between vertical steel mullions, and at several key points it extends up or down beyond the building portion it is enclosing, as if to make clear that it is not a structural wall, but a covering applied later. Every curtain wall is that, of course, but Piano here takes this classic element of Chicago postwar architecture, and exaggerates it with wit and compositional skill, at once paying his respects to the modern curtain wall and giving it a new twist (fig. 10).

The overall effect, as with almost all of Piano's buildings, is one of considerable lightness, but—and this, too, is always characteristic of Piano—never does the feeling of lightness spill over into flimsiness. This is no building that will look as if it might fly away in Chicago's lake-side winds, or as if it would be unable to hold its own beside the stone-clad wings that pre-ceded it. Once again, Piano's extraordinary sense of balance comes into play. The vertical ribs of the glass curtain wall give a light, almost delicate texture that breaks down the larger scale of the building. The stone, smooth and solid though still light in color, serves as a counter-point to the metal and glass. There is a huge, overhanging canopy of extruded aluminum, which Piano has called the "flying carpet," extending out beyond the eastern part of the structure on all four sides and supported by thin steel columns (fig. 11). From afar, it really does appear almost to float. ("I am simple enough to believe that making a roof is great art, but it is also the simple dream of shelter," Piano has said. "The idea of putting that roof up there, flying above the building—it is a shelter for art, a parasol, but also a shelter for life.")

The canopy, as Piano suggests, is both poem and prose. In effect a gigantic sunscreen, it is a descendant of the roof Piano used in the Agnelli rooftop gallery in Turin, as well as that of the Beyeler and, to a lesser extent, the Menil. In each case the roof contains fins, or blades, which capture north light and reflect it down into the galleries while blocking light from the south, east, or west (fig. 12). In Chicago, as in these earlier Piano museums, the canopy is both a key part of the process of controlling natural light in the galleries and a powerful visual composition in itself. Its broad overhang, which actually seems not so much to be flying as to be comfortably at rest, gives the structure a self-assured, rooted presence.

Since the late 1970s the northeast corner of the site had been defined largely by the use of the entry arch from Louis Sullivan's great Stock Exchange Building, here standing free as if it were a piece of monumental outdoor sculpture. With the angled entry to the Rubloff wing as its backdrop, the Art Institute provided a well-intentioned but somewhat graceless setting for the arch, which seemed to cry out for a door beneath it and a building above it. Obviously, Piano could not restore Sullivan's building, the demolition of which in 1972 remains one of the city's architectural tragedies, but he was able to give the arch a somewhat more dignified presence by aligning it to his façade and offering it, once again, at least some connection to an architectural context, however tenuous. (Piano himself could be said to deepen the tie between Sullivan and the Art Institute, at least conceptually, since there is something slightly Sullivan-like about the way in which Piano's work seems simultaneously delicate and robust.)

The three-story structure under Piano's flying roof, which contains new quarters for the museum's education program on the ground floor and the galleries for modern and contem-porary art on the two floors above, forms the main mass of the new wing as it will be seen from Millennium Park. It is roughly symmetrical, and can almost seem, from a distance, to have some of the characteristics of an Edward Durell Stone building from the 1960s—light, modern, determinedly not sleek in the manner of a Miesian building, and its symmetrical façade set underneath an oversized, overhanging roof supported by thin columns. When you get

figure 11
View, looking west, of the Modern Wing of the Art Institute, showing the "flying carpet" over the east pavilion and the Tom and Margot Pritzker Garden, June 2009.

closer, of course, you see that it is something else altogether: not warmed-over, slightly distorted classicism, but an inventive Modernism that does not hesitate to embrace symmetry when it seems appropriate—in this case, as a means of responding to Millennium Park but also as a way of providing some counterpoint to the disorder of the Skidmore, Owings & Merrill sections, which will now be largely hidden behind it.

Piano's aesthetic is in large part a story of inventive, elegant, and often subtle juxtapositions of materials, textures, and solids and voids as a means of achieving compositional balance. He likes complexity, and he likes ambiguity, and the notion that buildings reveal themselves in stages as you move toward them and through them. In the case of the façade of the Modern Wing, Piano's first surprise is that it is not nearly so reliant on symmetry as it first appears, since it turns out that the large, high symmetrical box that dominates the façade and sits below the flying roof structure is part of a larger composition. The high box, which contains the main galleries for contemporary and modern art, forms the eastern portion of Piano's new wing; beside it to the right is a smaller pavilion, the western portion of the wing, slightly lower and not covered by the flying roof structure. This western pavilion has additional galleries, including those for design and architecture, and small special exhibitions; meeting rooms for the Art Institute's Board of Trustees; dining facilities, with an adjacent outdoor terrace for sculpture; a museum shop; and a new entrance to the museum, replacing the present east entrance into the Rubloff wing from Columbus Drive.

This entry will lead directly into Piano's most important public space, a 300-foot-long, 30-foot-high, 30-foot-wide axis that extends southward to join the existing building. It is more than the main circulation spine for the Modern Wing; it is an interior public street for the entire museum, a place that, however great its collections and however pleasing some of its galleries, has never been clear in its layout, or had a corridor that functioned as a kind of "main street," a spine from which all other parts of the museum could be logically accessed (fig. 13). (The neatly ordered Rice Building is an exception to the general complexity, but to experience its clarity you have to get to it, which is not always easy or logical.)

figure 12
View, looking west, of the blades of the "flying carpet" over the Modern Wing, under construction, March 2008.

figure 13
Interior view, looking south, of
the Kenneth and Anne Griffin
Court, the principal north-south
axis of the Modern Wing of the
Art Institute, June 2009.

THE MODERN
WING
ARCHITECTURAL
PHOTOGRAPHY
PAUL
WARCHOL

Left
View of downtown Chicago, looking southwest, showing the Modern Wing of the Art Institute in relation to Grant Park, Millennium Park, and the city's historic skyline along and behind Michigan Avenue.

Following pages
View of the Monroe Street façade of the Modern Wing, as seen from underneath the Nichols Bridgeway.

103

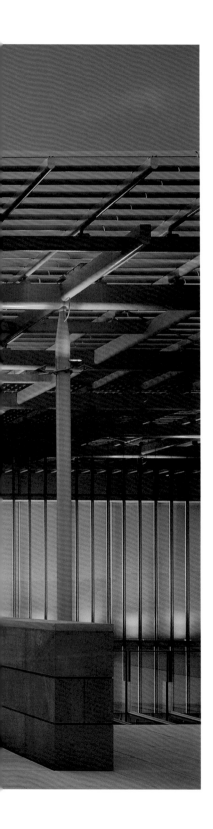

Left
The graceful profile of the Nichols Bridgeway has been compared to that of a racing shell.

Far left
Exterior view, looking north, showing the windows of the Terzo Piano restaurant at far left, and directly ahead, inside the building, the Gretchen and John Jordan II Terrace, which is adjacent to the third-floor galleries of modern European art.

Above, left and right
Views, looking north and east, of the Nichols Bridgeway and its junction with the third floor of the Modern Wing's west pavilion. Visible in the photograph at upper left are the two steel cantilevers that support the bridge at its south end.

Opposite page
The 620-foot-long Nichols Bridgeway descends in a gentle arc to Millennium Park and features a textured aluminum decking that will be heated in winter to keep it open and accessible to all visitors.

Left
View, looking southwest, from within the glass box on the west façade of the Modern Wing, high above the Metra rail tracks that run beneath the Art Institute.

Opposite page, top
The Bluhm Family Terrace, atop the third floor of the Modern Wing's west pavilion and adjacent to the Terzo Piano restaurant, is an open-air gallery overlooking Millennium Park and providing extraordinary views of the city's skyline. The 3,400-square-foot terrace will feature rotating exhibitions of contemporary sculpture.

Opposite page, bottom
Panoramic view, looking south, of the Art Institute, Grant Park, and Millennium Park, set between Lake Michigan and downtown Chicago.

Opposite page
Detail views of the entrance
to the galleries of contemporary
art and of the glass side walls
and oak-trimmed handrails of the
stairs between the second and
third floors.

Above
Interior view of the third-floor landing
at the north end of the Jordan
Terrace, one of two suspended
walkways (or *passerelles*) in the
east pavilion of the Modern Wing.

Above: Interior view from Griffin Court of the Monroe Street entrance to the Modern Wing, the suspended staircase and *passerelle*, and the entrance to the Pritzker Garden.

Above
The double glass curtain wall along the north façade of the Modern Wing insulates the galleries of the east pavilion, while providing a dramatic connection with Millennium Park.

Opposite page
In conjunction with the "flying carpet" overhead, the third-floor skylights and the velum-panel ceiling create an ideal environment for viewing the masterpieces in the museum's collection of modern European art.

Above, left and right
Galleries throughout the Modern Wing, such as these on the third floor devoted to 20th-century European art, employ a demountable wall system designed by Renzo Piano.

Opposite page
The Department of Contemporary Art uses the Albert A. Robin Family Galleries—comprising the Muriel Kallis Steinberg Newman Gallery, the Alfred L. and Nancy Lauter McDougal Gallery, and the Karla Scherer Gallery—largely for the display of art from the postwar period through the 1960s.

Above and opposite page
The second-floor galleries of contemporary art in the east pavilion feature precast concrete beams that provide a floor-to-ceiling height of just over eighteen feet. Within these galleries several customized rooms have been created expressly for the in-depth display of works by particular artists.

SELECTIONS
FROM THE
ARCHITECTURE
AND
DESIGN
COLLECTION

Opposite page
The Department of Architecture and Design now has at its disposal approximately 8,000 square feet of space for the display of its permanent holdings within the Temple Smith and Esther Smith Family Gallery and the Harold and Margot Schiff Gallery.

Above
The Carolyn S. and Matthew Bucksbaum Gallery provides space for the Department of Photography within the Modern Wing.

Above, left and right
Interior views of the "west box" containing the escalator and elevator that provide access to and from the Nichols Bridge-way, the Terzo Piano restaurant, and the Bluhm Family Terrace.

Above, left and right
Views from above the glass curtain wall down into the Tom and Margot Pritzker Garden and the Anne Searle Bent Terrace. Altogether, the Pritzker Garden, the Brooks McCormick Court, and the BP Student Esplanade increase the museum's green space by over 21,000 square feet.

Opposite page
Interior view of the bright flooring and warm birch-veneer paneling and doors within the Patrick G. and Shirley W. Ryan Education Center.

Above, left and right
Among the facilities in the new Ryan Education Center are, clockwise from upper left, the Searle Funds at the Chicago Community Trust Classroom, the David and Marilyn Fatt Vitale Family Orientation Room, and the Elizabeth Morse Studio.

Above
View of the north end of the 620-foot-long Nichols Bridge-way as it touches down inside Millennium Park.

Opposite page
Interspersed with exterior views of the Modern Wing are interiors of the Nichols Board of Trustees Suite, the Terzo Piano restaurant, and the Modern Shop.

Above, left and right
Views, looking east, of the "flying carpet" over the east pavilion of the Modern Wing and the Tom and Margot Pritzker Garden.

Opposite page
View from the Anne Searle Bent Terrace into the Pritzker Garden, showing Ellsworth Kelly's *White Curve*, commissioned in honor of former director James N. Wood.

Above and opposite page
Views of the Monroe Street façade of the Modern Wing of the Art Institute.

Left
View, looking southeast, of the Art Institute of Chicago, Grant Park, and Lake Michigan.

PROJECT DRAWINGS ELEVATIONS, SECTIONS, AND PLANS RENZO PIANO BUILDING WORKSHOP

Above
Monroe Street (north) elevation
of the Modern Wing, with a view
of the renovated north façade
of Gunsaulus Hall.

Preceding spread (p. 136)
Partial north-south section through
the first-floor Ryan Education
Center and the second- and third-
floor galleries of the east pavilion
of the Modern Wing.

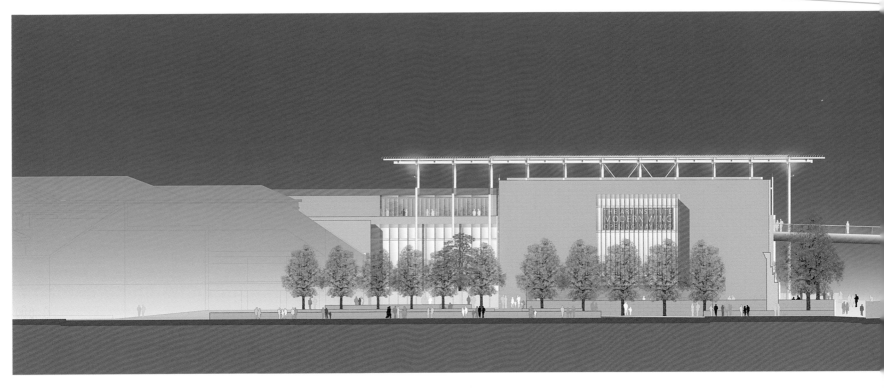

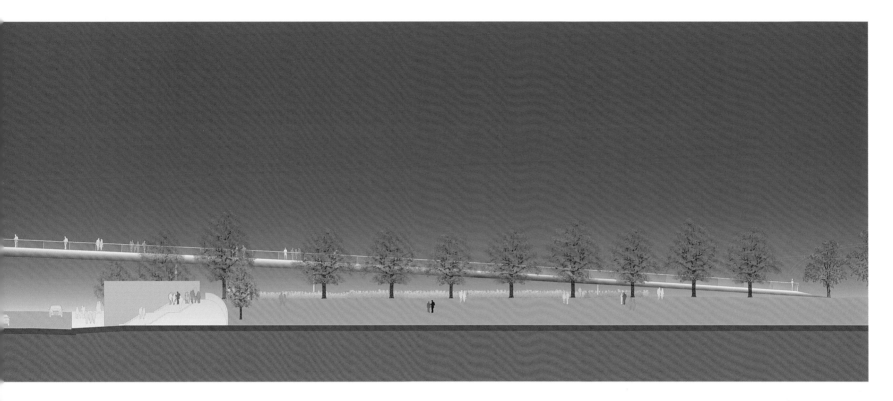

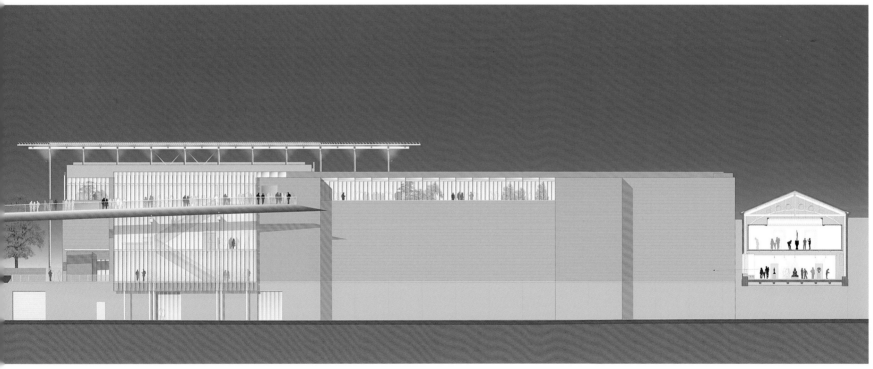

Top: Columbus Drive (east) elevation of the Modern Wing and the Nichols Bridgeway.

Above: West elevation, with a section through Gunsaulus Hall.

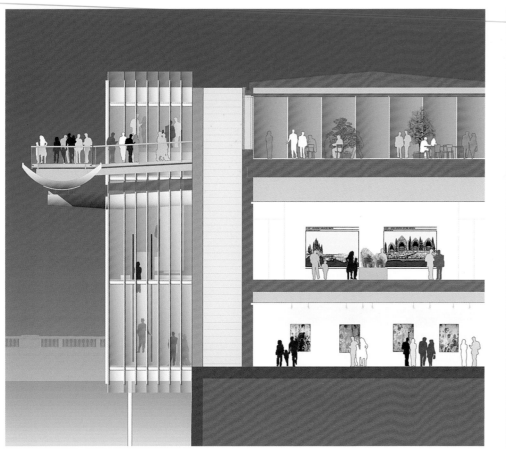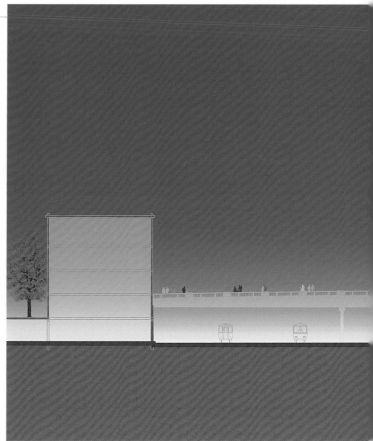

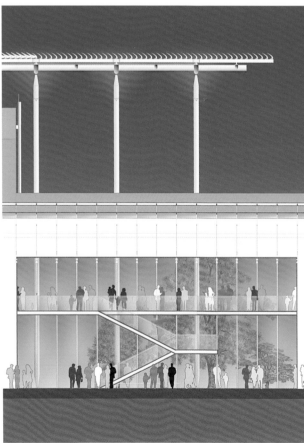

Above and opposite page, top
East-west transverse sectional view through the Modern Wing and the Pritzker Garden, with a detail view of the first-floor Abbott Galleries for special exhibitions, the second-floor Temple Smith and Esther Smith Family Gallery for the Department of Architecture and Design, and the third-floor Terzo Piano restaurant.

Left and far left
North-south longitudinal section through the Griffin Court of the Modern Wing, with a detail view of the *passerelle* and staircase, and the "flying carpet" over the Pritzker Garden.

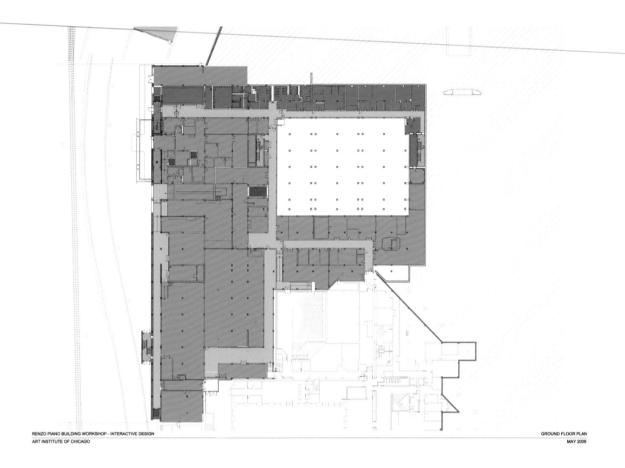

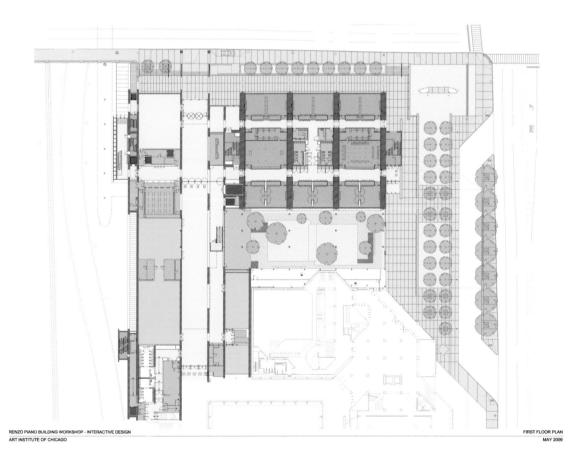

Top and left
Ground-floor and first-floor plans,
respectively, of the Modern Wing.

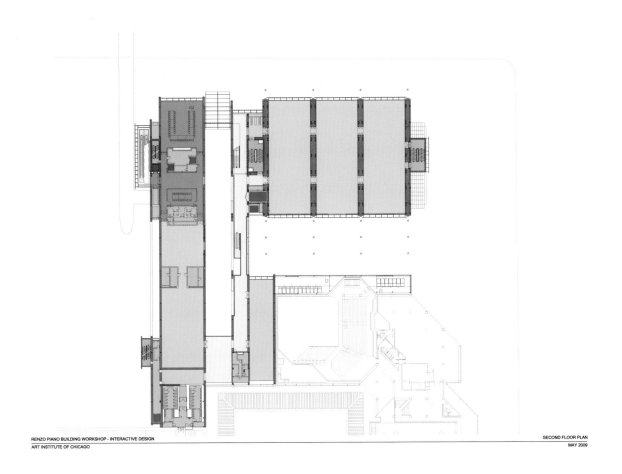

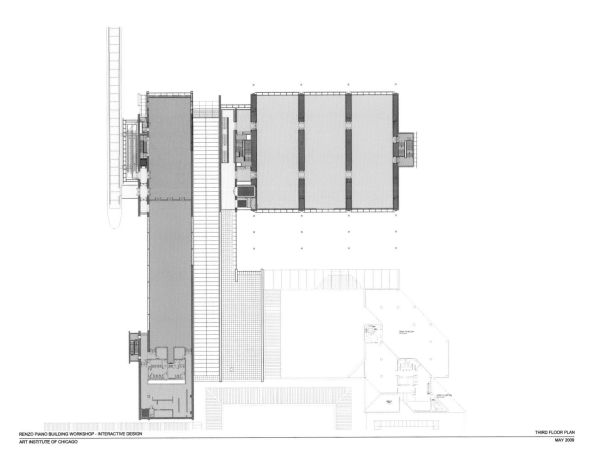

Top and left
Second-floor and third-floor plans, respectively, of the Modern Wing.

ACKNOWLEDGMENTS
RECOGNIZING THOSE WHO MADE IT POSSIBLE

BUILDING OF THE CENTURY CAMPAIGN

Contributions as of July 31, 2009

The Building of the Century Campaign ranks as the most successful fund-raising effort ever undertaken by a Chicago cultural institution. At the time of the Modern Wing's civic dedication on May 16, 2009, the museum had secured more than $412 million for the design, construction, and endowment of this landmark addition and related capital projects. The success of the Modern Wing and the campaign are a testament to the leadership and vision of the Art Institute's Board of Trustees, the dedication of the capital campaign committee members, and the inspiring generosity of Chicago's philanthropic community.

At the Modern Wing's groundbreaking in May 2005, John H. Bryan, who was then chairman of the board, spoke to the importance of this addition: "The expansion of the Art Institute of Chicago heralds a new and exciting era in the history of the museum, bringing together the extraordinary vision of internationally renowned architect Renzo Piano and that of one of the nation's most beloved and respected cultural institutions." The bold plan for the Modern Wing inspired everyone who followed its growth, and the completed building has been enthusiastically embraced by the city of Chicago.

The Modern Wing is an addition built for generations. Fittingly, the museum recognizes the leading donors to the capital campaign as the Founders and Benefactors of the Art Institute of Chicago for the Twenty-First Century. The designation of Founders and Benefactors harkens back to Chicago's early philanthropists. Building on the legacy of their predecessors, today's Founders and Benefactors have secured the continued success of the Art Institute as one of the world's premier encyclopedic museums. We are pleased and proud to acknowledge these donors in the pages of this book as well as in Griffin Court, where they will be recognized in perpetuity for their unrivalled civic commitment.

We are likewise deeply grateful for the generosity of the Woman's Board, the Auxiliary Board, the Leadership Advisory Committee, the Evening Associates, and the Community Associates. These boards and museum affiliates came forward to give additional support for the Modern Wing above and beyond what they provide the Art Institute on an annual basis.

Leading corporations and foundations joined this remarkable effort as well. Their contributions are an investment in the cultural life of the city and an affirmation of the special role the Art Institute has in the lives of Chicagoans.

As we celebrate the Modern Wing—an historic addition to the Art Institute and to the city of Chicago—we would like to thank and recognize all of the donors who have made gifts in support of the Building of the Century Campaign.

Thomas J. Pritzker
Chairman
Board of Trustees

Louis B. Susman
Chairman, Building of the Century Campaign
Ambassador to the United Kingdom
of Great Britain and Northern Ireland

FOUNDERS OF THE ART INSTITUTE
OF CHICAGO FOR THE 21ST CENTURY
$15,000,000 and above
Anonymous
Marilynn B. Alsdorf
Kenneth C. and Anne D. Griffin
Eloise W. Martin
Alexandra C. and John D. Nichols

FOUNDERS OF THE ART INSTITUTE
OF CHICAGO FOR THE 21ST CENTURY
$10,000,000 to $14,999,999
The Bluhm Family
   Neil G. Bluhm
   Barbara Bluhm-Kaul
   Leslie Bluhm
   Andrew Bluhm
   Meredith Bluhm Wolf
BP Foundation
Gary C. and Frances Comer
The Harris Family Foundation,
   in Memory of Bette and Neison Harris
Chauncey and Marion D. McCormick
   Family Foundation
Pritzker Foundation and
   Margot and Thomas J. Pritzker
   Foundation

FOUNDERS OF THE ART INSTITUTE
OF CHICAGO FOR THE 21ST CENTURY
$5,000,000 to $9,999,999
Abbott
Anne Searle Bent
Mr. and Mrs. John H. Bryan
The Matthew and Carolyn S. Bucksbaum
   Family Foundation
Mr. and Mrs. Wesley M. Dixon, Jr.
Janet and Craig Duchossois
Fred Eychaner and Yang Guo
Richard and Mary L. Gray
JPMorgan Chase & Co.
Carol and Larry Levy Family
The Regenstein Foundation
Patrick G. and Shirley W. Ryan
The Earl and Brenda Shapiro Family
Mr. and Mrs. Roger L. Weston

BENEFACTORS OF THE ART INSTITUTE
OF CHICAGO FOR THE 21ST CENTURY
$1,000,000 to $4,999,999
Anonymous (4)
Bank of America
Marjorie and Martin R. Binder
Mr. and Mrs. Henry Buchbinder
Linda and Vincent Buonanno
Chicago Park District
The Clinton Family
The Crown Family
Shawn M. Donnelley and Christopher M. Kelly
The Edwardson Family Foundation
Mr. and Mrs. Marshall Field
Sylvia Neil and Daniel Fischel
Ginny and Peter Foreman
Barbara E. and Richard J. Franke
The Glasser and Rosenthal Family
Goldman, Sachs & Co.
Andrea and James Gordon
The Grainger Foundation
David and Mary Winton Green
Samuel and M. Patricia Grober
Diane and David B Heller
Illinois Tool Works Foundation
Martha Jacobshagen
Mr. and Mrs. John W. Jordan II
Rita and James Knox
Kay and Fred Krehbiel
The Kresge Foundation
Lavin Family Foundation
Liz and Eric Lefkofsky
Diane v. S. and Robert M. Levy
Julius Lewis and The Rhoades Foundation
The John D. and Catherine T. MacArthur
   Foundation
Mazza Foundation
McCormick Foundation
Alfred L. and Nancy Lauter McDougal
The Andrew W. Mellon Foundation
Ann and Samuel M. Mencoff
The Elizabeth Morse Charitable Trust
The Neisser Family
Muriel Kallis Steinberg Newman
Cynthia and Terry Perucca
Sidney L. Port
Anne and Chris Reyes
Betsy Bergman Rosenfield and
   Andrew M. Rosenfield

Karla Scherer
Mr. and Mrs. Harold Schiff
Daniel C. Searle
Searle Funds at the Chicago
   Community Trust
George and Joan Segal
Howard and Martha Simpson
Edward Byron Smith Family and
   E. B. and Maureen Smith Family
State of Illinois
Manfred and Fern Steinfeld
The Irving Stenn, Jr. Family
Howard S. Stone and Donna A. Stone
Marjorie and Louis B. Susman
Mr. and Mrs. Byron D. Trott
David and Marilyn Fatt Vitale
The Woman's Board of the Art Institute
   of Chicago
Mrs. William Wood Prince and Prince
   Charitable Trusts
Estate of Elouise B. Woods

Far left, above: Former Chairman of the Board of Trustees John H. Bryan, Maggie Daley, former director James N. Wood, President and Eloise W. Martin Director James Cuno, and Louis B. Susman, Chairman of the Building of the Century Campaign, at the ground-breaking ceremony for the Modern Wing, May 31, 2005.

Far left, below: Stephanie Comer with trustee Francie Comer.

Left, above: Trustee Janet Duchossois and Craig Duchossois on the Bluhm Family Terrace during the May 16, 2009, dedication ceremonies.

Left, below: Trustee Brenda Shapiro pictured with her sisters Lisa Goldfarb (left) and Mary Anne Lewis (right).

Far left, above: Andrew and Amy Bluhm, life trustees Wesley M. Dixon, Jr., and Neil Bluhm, and Margot Pritzker view a model of the Modern Wing with Douglas Druick, Searle Chair of Medieval through Modern European Painting and Sculpture and Prince Trust Chair of Prints and Drawings.

Far left, below: Life trustee Marilynn Alsdorf, Mary L. Gray, James Cuno, and life trustee Richard Gray gather following a talk by James Cuno and Renzo Piano on the Modern Wing, spring 2008.

Left, above: Mayor Richard M. Daley, Chairman of the Board of Trustees Thomas J. Pritzker, past chairman John Nichols, trustee Alexandra Nichols, and architect Renzo Piano at the dedication of the Nichols Bridgeway, May 16, 2009.

Left, below: Margot Pritzker, Chairman of the Board of Trustees Thomas J. Pritzker, President and Eloise W. Martin Director James Cuno, Sarah Stewart, Maggie Daley, Mayor Richard M. Daley, Anne Griffin, and trustee Kenneth Griffin at the Woman's Board gala, May 9, 2009.

Far left: Renzo Piano addresses a crowd of museum supporters at the civic dedication of the Modern Wing on May 16, 2009. Seated on the dais behind him are White House Chief of Staff Rahm Emanuel, Mayor Richard M. Daley, past chairman John H. Bryan, President and Eloise W. Martin Director James Cuno, Chairman of the Board of Trustees Thomas J. Pritzker, and Chicago Park District Commissioner Rouhy Shalabi.

Middle, above: Trustee and cochair Caryn Harris and King Harris at the Modern Wing opening gala.

Middle, below: Margot and Thomas J. Pritzker in the Pritzker Garden.

Right, above: Corbett Ryan, trustee Shirley Welsh Ryan, and Patrick G. Ryan dedicate the Ryan Education Center.

Right, below: William M. Daley, chairman of the midwest region for JPMorgan Chase & Co., Founding Civic Sponsor of the Modern Wing, joins James Cuno for an inspection of the building site in spring 2007.

Far left: Griffin Court was filled with guests during the opening gala.

Left: Carol Levy and trustee Lawrence Levy at the Modern Wing opening gala on May 9, 2009.

Above: Don Kaul and trustee Barbara Bluhm-Kaul talk with Ellsworth Kelly in the Pritzker Garden.

THE SUSTAINING FELLOWS AND
THE BUILDING OF THE CENTURY CAMPAIGN

The Art Institute of Chicago is honored to recognize the extraordinary generosity of the Sustaining Fellows to the Building of the Century Campaign.

Founded in 1977 as the museum's premier donor society, the Sustaining Fellows provide unrestricted contributions that help ensure that the Art Institute's collections, exhibitions, and educational programs are of the highest caliber. The Sustaining Fellows responded to the Building of the Century campaign with broad and deep support above and beyond their annual commitment to the museum. In recognition of this generosity, the Sustaining Fellows Gallery on the Modern Wing's third floor was dedicated in their honor.

The Art Institute is proud to acknowledge as Sustaining Fellows Gallery Sponsors those members who made campaign contributions of $100,000 or more.

The museum is likewise grateful to acknowledge as Modern Fellows those members who made campaign contributions of $25,000 to $99,999.

SUSTAINING FELLOWS
GALLERY SPONSORS
$100,000 and above
Anonymous
Mr. and Mrs. Thomas S.
    Alexander
Mr. and Mrs. Walter Alexander
Jill and Richard Almeida
Marilynn B. Alsdorf
Mary and Paul Anderson
Mrs. Roger Allen Anderson
Ann and Bruce Bachmann
Mr. and Mrs. Robert H. Bacon
Caroline and John Ballantine
Mr. and Mrs. Walter F. Bandi
Julie and Roger Baskes
Anne Searle Bent
Jean and John Berghoff
Marie Krane Bergman and
    Robert H. Bergman
Harriet and Harry Bernbaum
Marjorie and Martin R. Binder
The Bluhm Family
    Neil G. Bluhm
    Barbara Bluhm-Kaul
    Leslie Bluhm

Andrew Bluhm
    Meredith Bluhm Wolf
Mr. and Mrs. John H. Bryan
Mr. and Mrs. Henry Buchbinder
Scott, Lynda, Jonathan &
    Lindsey Canel
The Matthew and Carolyn S.
    Bucksbaum Family Foundation
Linda and Vincent Buonanno
Mrs. Silas S. Cathcart
Joyce Chelberg
Marcia S. Cohn
Mr. and Mrs. E. David Coolidge III
Nancy Raymond Corral
The Crown Family
Mr. and Mrs. Wesley M. Dixon, Jr.
Janet and Craig Duchossois
The Edwardson Family
    Foundation
Efroymson Family Fund,
    a CICF Fund
Enivar Charitable Fund
Joan and Robert Feitler and
    the Smart Family Foundation
Harve A. Ferrill
Mr. and Mrs. Marshall Field

Ginny and Peter Foreman
Lynn and Jim, Craig, Kyle,
    and Kim Foster
Mike and David W. Fox
Barbara E. and
    Richard J. Franke
Mr. and Mrs. Maurice F. Fulton
Wilbur H. and Linda T. Gantz
Virginia and Gary Gerst
The Glasser and Rosenthal
    Family
Ethel and William Gofen
Helyn S. Goldenberg and
    Michael N. Alper
Richard and Mary L. Gray
David and Mary Winton Green
Kenneth C. and Anne D. Griffin
Mr. and Mrs. John P. Grube
Evangeline R. Haarlow and
    the Haarlow Family
    Charitable Foundation
Mr. and Mrs. Charles C.
    Haffner III
The Harris Family Foundation,
    in Memory of Bette and
    Neison Harris

Diane and David B Heller
Mr. and Mrs. David C. Hilliard
Mary P. Hines
Doris and Marshall Holleb
Karen and Tom Howell
Pamela K. and Roger B. Hull
The Jentes Family
Mr. and Mrs. John W. Jordan II
Burt and Anne Kaplan
Dolores Kohl Kaplan and
    Morris A. Kaplan
Alyce K. Sigler and
    Stephen A. Kaplan
Judy and John Keller
Phil and Judy Kirk and
    The Kirk Foundation
Rita and James Knox
Anne T. and W. Paul Krauss
Anne and Robert Krebs
Kay and Fred Krehbiel
Lavin Family Foundation
Liz and Eric Lefkofsky
Harry and Betty Levin
Elaine and Donald
    Levinson
Diane v. S. and Robert M. Levy

Julius Lewis and
    The Rhoades Foundation
Renée Logan
Josephine and John J. Louis
    Foundation
Susan and Lewis Manilow
Mr. and Mrs. John F. Manley
Robert and Ellen Marks
Chauncey and Marion D.
    McCormick Family
    Foundation
Judith and Howard McCue
Alfred L. and
    Nancy Lauter McDougal
Patty and Mark McGrath
Cheryl and Eric McKissack
Rande and Cary McMillan
Edward and Lucy R. Minor and
    the Edward and Lucy R.
    Minor Family Foundation
Stuart D. and Nancie Mishlove
Diana and David Moore
The Neisser Family
Muriel Kallis Steinberg Newman
Alexandra C. and John D. Nichols
Irma Parker

Left: James Cuno leads Sustaining Fellows on a hard-hat tour of Griffin Court and the Modern Wing in the fall of 2007.

Far left, above: James Cuno leads Sustaining Fellows Mack Trapp, Terry and Cynthia Perucca, Carol Trapp, Anne Krebs, and Rose Shure on a hard-hat tour of the Modern Wing construction site.

Far left, below: Trustee Rita Knox, William Sick, and Stephanie Sick, President of the Sustaining Fellows, at the Woman's Board gala for *Jasper Johns: Gray*.

Left, above: Mark and Patty McGrath with Program Committee Chairman Jean Berghoff and John Berghoff at a Sustaining Fellows dinner honoring Ed Ruscha.

Left, below: Sustaining Fellows Chairman Barbara Franke, Ellsworth Kelly, Maureen Smith, and trustee E. B. Smith, Jr., at the Modern Wing groundbreaking ceremony.

Far left, above: Trustee Julius Lewis with Abby McCormick O'Neil and D. Carroll Joynes.

Far left, below: Robert O. Delaney and life trustees Quinn Delaney and Wesley M. Dixon, Jr.

Left: Grant McCullagh with trustee Anne Searle Bent, Anne Vogt Fuller and Marion Titus Searle Curator of Prints and Drawings Suzanne Folds McCullagh, and Stephen P. Bent.

Above: Trustee Roger Weston and Pamela Weston at the Modern Wing opening gala.

Eric Abaka
Katie Abascal
Henry Abboud
Yamilett Abejon
Richard Acosta
Kenyata Adams
Shirley Adams
Edward Adams, Jr.
Eugene Adams, Jr.
Elizabeth Adamsick
Mark Adkins
Maude Afful House
Charlene Agabao
Felipe Aguilar, Jr.
Rosamond Agyeman
Barbara Ahlberg
Dina Ahsmann
Alexander Airey
Mary Albert
Dianne Albin
Christina Alexander
John Alexander
William Alexander
James Allan
Amy Allen
Brooke Allen
Bruce Allen
Hilda Allen
Jason Allen
Andre Allen, Jr.
Kenneth Alvarez
Sarah Alvarez
Sarvenaz Amanat
Lindsay Amini
Robert Andersen
David Anderson
Hale Anderson
Jennifer Anderson
Laura Anderson
Marjorie Anderson
Terrance Anderson
Willie Anderson
Delaus Anderson, Jr.

Janeiro Andres
Margaret Annett
Laticia Annison-Romano
Barbara Ansell
Eric Anyah
Steven Archer
Juan Arellano
Casey Arling
Cheryl Arvio
Rodrigo Arzaluz
Shakari Asbury
Derome Ashford
Sandra Ashman
Pomi Assefa
Kamera Aton
Casey Attale
Mike Attig
Elizabeth Auer
Susan Augustine
Eusebio Avitia
Amy Babinec
Irene Backus
David Baggett
Dawn Baggett
Katherine Bahr
De'Andre Bailey
Andrea Bainbridge
Renee Bair
Daniel Baird
Devon Baker
Rochelle Baker
Russell Baker
Edwin Balcita
Francesca Baldry
Kathryn Baldwin
Elizabeth Balik
Dennis Ball
James Ballen
Amy Ballmer
Jennifer Balton
Julia Banderas
Geraldine Banik
Jerry Banks

Ruth Barabe
Yevgeniya Baras
Carl Baratta
Michael Barber
Ana Barbus
Brandon Barnes
Thomas Barnes
Jonnie Barnes-Sanford
Oscar Barraza
Donald Barrett
Nicholas Barron
Heather Barrow
Scott Barsotti
Judith Barter
Kyle Bartholomew
Raoul Vic Basa
William Basanise
Irena Basiura
Kim Baskin
Rene Batres
Barbara Battaglia
Ray Battle
Jessica Batty
Betty Baugh
Deborah Baugh
Kathryn Baum
Denise Bautista
Maritza Bautista
Susan Bazargan
Brian Beard
Brianna Beard
Son Beattie
Kevin Beck
Dorinda Bedar
Amanda Beechy
Robin Beeson
Nancy Behall
Kathleen Bejma
Albert Belcher
Melissa Bell
Colisha Belmont
John Bembenek
Melinda Bennett

Ramon Berber
Jelena Berenc
Cherish Berg
Bernard Berger
Jessica Berger
Sherri Berger
Amy Berman
David Bernard
Emma Bernstein
David Berry
Kathleen Berzock
Heather Bezdecheck
Aniko Bezur
Dave Bhagwandin
Dyna Bieber
Gregory Bieniek
Donald Bieszczak
Atiqah Binbek
Michael Bingaman
Matthew Bisbey
Crystal Bishop
Colin Bishopp
James Bittner
Andrew Blackley
Caren Blackmore
Matthew Blake
Samuel Blanchard
Peter Blank
Shanta Blanton
Julie Blecker
Jonathan Bloomer
Michael Blossom
Stephanie Blue
Krystal Bobbett
Samatha Bodanapu
Olenka Bodnarskyj
Mary Boetto
Juliet Bonczkowski
Veronica Bond
Yolanda Bonds
Matthew Bonnette
Dorothy Booker
Kristal Booker

Shelly Booker
Keith Boone
Melonie Boone
Thomas Bosworth
Bruce Boucher
William Bourland
Marine Bouvier
Sylvia Bouye-Roberson
Tamiko Bowie
Marjorie Bowker
E. Boyd
Madina Boyd
Lori Boyer
Elizabeth Boyne
Mia Boyson
Henry Bracy
Catherine Bradley
Miriam Braganza
Neal Brailov
Hilary Branch
Pamela Brandt
Jeremy Brantley
Jennifer Breckner
Jennifer Breen
Donna Brennan
Jameel Brewer
Ashley Brice
Raymonde Brice
Christine Brindle
Clare Britt
Jill Britton
Charron Brock
Kristin Brockman
Jason Brogan
Russell Brohl
Christopher Brooks
Amber Brown
Andrew Brown
Billy Brown
Charles Brown
Clarissa Brown
Debra Brown
Jack Brown

Joshua Brown	Nathan Carder	Caesar Citraro	Sarah Coulter	Cristina De Guia
Kelly Brown	Anahi Cardona	Dennis Clar	Angela Cox	Robert De Jesus
Marlon Brown	Peter Cardone	Markeshia Clark	Craig Cox	Emilie DeAngelis
Maxwell Brown	Katherine Cares	Cynthia Clarke	John Cox	Lawrence Del Pilar
Rory Brown	Susan Carlson	Jane Clarke	John Craig	Eddy Del Real
Steven Brown	Raymond Carlson, Jr.	Jay Clarke	Karen Craig	Ricky Del Rosario
Tanya Brown-Merriman	Citlali Carrillo	Emily Clary	Cassandra Crawford	Lizette Del Toro
Adrienne Buchholz	Jeffrey Carrillo	Judi Claxton	Marion Crawford	Lyn Delliquadri
Lucas Bucholtz	Catherine Carroll	Emily Clayton	William Cribbs	Emily Derse
Jill Bugajski	Colleen Carroll	Anne Cleavenger	Jessica Crippen	Nina Dew
Melissa Bugajski	Laurie Carroll	Michelle Cleek	Lisa Cromartie	Anna Di Cesare
Lara Bullock	Faybian Carter	Breanne Clifton	Joel Cronkite	Celeste Diaz
Katie Bunch	Francesca Casadio	Emily Cobb	Mary Ann Crotty	Patricia Dickerson
Katherine Bunker	Sally Casillo	Mark Cobb	Amber Crouch	Jonathan Dickert
Anthony Bunting	Martha Castro	Myeshia Cobbs	Dennis Crow	Karla Dickert
Corey Burage	Margaret Catania	Cynthia Cochand	Christopher Crowder	Joseph Dickinson
Lisa Burback	Hillary Catrow	Joseph Cochand	Andrea Crump	Loni Diep
Brittany Burcham	Michael Cavanagh	Patricia Cogan	Alethea Cruz	George Dimis
Rebecca Burditt	Herman Ceasar	Maria Coker	Ramona Cruz	Joseph Dishmon, Jr.
Darren Burge	Kristin Ceto	Edward Cole	Salvador Cruz	Mary Diskin
Gaylene Burger	Shaw-Jiun Chalitsios-Wang	Rachel Martin Cole	Brandy Culp	Anthony Dixon
Elijah Burgher	Benjamin Chambers	Johnny Coleman	Chelsea Culp	Makeba Dixon-Hill
Elliot Burin	Anne Champagne	Megan Coleman	Kathleen Cummings	Kyle Doering
Amanda Burk	Lauren Chang	Jessica Collier	James Cunningham	Jennifer Dohm
Lauren Burke	Michaelanne Chapel	Andey Collins	James Cuno	Markus Dohner
Melanie Burke	Jerrel Chapman	Duane Collins	James Currie	Cengiz Dokumaci
Philip Burke	Sara Chapman	Geauna Collins	Kenneth Curtis	Emily Doman
Katherine Burnett	Cheri Charlton	Lawrie Mae Coloma	Jessica Cybulski	Alberto Dominguez
Libby Burnette	Julie Charmelo-Nguyen	Sarah-Emma Colon	James Czarney	Eltonio Donaldson
Robert Burnier	Tara Charney	Allison Condo	Mariusz Czyz	Nicholas Donnelly
Ryan Burns	James Charnot	Albertine Conell	Lisa D'Acquisto	Michael Donovan
Katherine Bussard	Natdrina Chatman	Christine Conniff-O'Shea	Kristi Dahm	Susan Donovan
Judy Butler	Erick Chavez	James Connolly	Elizabeth Dalal	Lisa Dorin
Jennifer Butterfield	Aprajita Chawla	Margarita Connors	Stephanie D'Alessandro	Julius Dorsey III
Ryan Butterfield	Meira Chefitz	Joelle Contorno	Dawn Dalle Molle	Christina Dougherty
Emily Butwin	Yan Nan Chen	Benjamin Cook	Yvonne Daniels	Jessica Downing
Tristan Bynum	Yu Cheng	Hillary Cook	Rena Dantzler	Travis Downs
Patrick Byrnes	Anne Chernik	Lasha Cook	Regina Darby	Bryan Drake
Carmen Caballero	Lindsay Chick	Ruth Cook	Paul Davies	Rachel Drescher
William Caddick	Yen Shi Chin	Stefanie Cook	Charles Davis	Frank Drew
Montelle Cade	Laurie Chipps	Melissa Coon	Darrow Davis	Emmet Drews
Greg Cahillane	Vinod Chopra	Daniel Coonfield	Devin Davis	Mary Jane Drews
Perry Caldwell	Brooke Christensen	Bernadine Cooper	Julie Davis	Cheryl Dring
Kevin Calus	Jason Christensen	David Corbett	LaKeisha Davis	Joe Driver
Charles Campbell	Janet Christiansen	Will Macon Cordier	Lauren Davis	Tracey Drobot
Erik Campbell	Bernice Chu	Jamiel Cornelio	Warren Davis	Matthew Drogo
Megan Campbell	Dorota Chudzicka	Quirino Corona	Consuela Dawson	Douglas Druick
Gregory Cannon	John Cichon	Christine Coscioni	Titus Dawson	Helen Drysdale
Luis Cantoral	Pamela Cipkowski	Heather Costello	Jeremy Day	Jennifer Dudzienski
Emily Capper	David Ciske	Katherine Costin	Alison De Frank	Vautralise Dunlap

Jeanne Ladd	Towana Lewis	Estera Manikowska	Megan McGee	Patricia Mocco
Vanessa Lagrone	Zachary Lewis	Lanette Manley	Esau McGhee	Dorothea Moeller
Margaret Laing	Jennifer Li	Lola Mann	Kathleen McGovern	Whitney Moeller
Hue Lam	Adam Lieb	Tonya Manney	Ciara McGreevy	Joseph Mohan
Nora Lambert	Shannon Liedel	Julian Manning	Michelle McGuire	Kathryn Moioli
Dana Lamparello	Robert Lifson	Shaun Manning	Mary McInnis	John Molini
Marvin Landrum	Sheena Lilly	Rebecca Manuel	Annette McIntee	Christopher Monkhouse
Elizabeth Lane	Nancy Lim	Maria Marable-Bunch	Molly McKenzie	Janell Monson
Matthew Lane	Grace Lin	Brooke Markovitch	Freddie McKinley	Sandra Montgomery
Allison Langley	Anne Lindberg	Alexis Marlin	Jack McLaughlin	Alberto Montoya
David Langley	Kevin Lint	Aimee Marshall	Brendan McMahon	Hope Moody
George Langlois	Kristin Lister	Melanie Marshall	Michael McNamara	Monica Moody
Maren Lankford	Edward Little	Dominique Martin	Robert McNay	Darci Mooney
Amey Larmore	Michael Litzenberg	George Martin	Denise McNease	Carl Moore
Sean Laseter	Lucas Livingston	Rebecca Martin	Julie Mech	Colonell Moore
June Lashley	David Lloyd	Cesar Martinez	Jamie Medeiros	Iris Moore
Elaine Laslie	Meredith Lockridge	Cyrus Martinez	Mei Mei	James Moore
Brian Laster	Jennifer Lockwood	Diego Martinez	Janette Mejia	Jocelyn Moralde
Katie Latham	Patricia Loiko	Jaime Martinez	Dolores Melendez	Michelle Morales
Julie Lawrenz	Brenda London-Tate	Julian Martinez	Nancy Melin	Aliza Morell
Patricia Lawson	Tommijo Loudermilk	Lulu Martinez	Renee Melton	Christopher Morgan
Elliot Layda	Andrew Loughnane	Miriam Martinez	Kenneth Menclewicz	Lindsay Morgan
Edward Layne	Nina Love	Nicholas Marzullo	Melissa Mendez	Matthew Morley
Qi Le	Nenette Luarca	Kimberly Masius	Robyn Mertel	Marcia Morrell
Shalini Le Gall	James Lucas	Perry Mason	Gabor Meszaros	Alina Morris
Anna LeBlanc	Boris Lucero	Alice Masse	Susan Meyer	Carrie Morris
Rebecca Lederman	Stefan Lucke	Leslie Mastroianni	Thomas Meyers	Dominic Morris
Carol Lee	Susan Luisi	Elizabeth Mather	Hannah Michaelson	Erika Morris
Catherine Lee	Meredith Lusher	Jesse Mathes	Paulette Michel	Ian Morrison
Chia Lee	Aisha Luster	Tricia Mathews	Joel Midden	Jo-Ann Morrison
Edna Lee	Margaret Lynch	Aleksandra Matic	Jonas Middleton	Linda Morrison
Hyun Lee	Matthew Lynch	Lilita Matison	Emily Mihalik	Angela Morrow
Larry Lee	Donovan Lyons	Margalit Matso	Michael Milano	Anne Morse
Linda Lee	Laverne Lyons	Michael Maurello	Diane Miliotes	Terrance Mosby
Phil Lee	Marilyn Mabra	Timothy Mayse-Lillig	Bryan Miller	Aurelia Moser
Rainer Lee	Meredith Mack	Kenia Mazier	Colleen Miller	Aime Moussambote
Yeo Woon Lee	Darret Maddox	Craig McBride	Erma Miller	Sara Moy
Janet Lefley	Pascual Madrigal	Alison McCarty	Kaitlyn Miller	Laura Mueller
John Lehrman	Denise Mahoney	Lisa McCaskill	Laura Miller	Samaiyah Muhammad-Wright
Michelle Lehrman Jenness	Shirley Mahoney	Denise McCaster	Norma Miller	
Jamal Leki Albano	Matthew Majer	Jonathan McClellan	Tasha Miller	Kimberley Muir
Justin Lemberg	Erin Makowski	Petra McClure	Tyrone Miller	Justine Mullen
Ashley Lerner	Stephanie Maldonado	Wilbur McCord	Sidney Mills	Shirley Mullens
Kevin Less	Jacqueline Maman	Jessica McCormack	Thomas Minota	Arturo Muneton, Jr.
Floree Lesure	Regina Mamou	Jeraldine McCormick	Anya Mitchell	Maria Murguia
Alexandra Letvin	Jean Manayala	Maceo McCray	Michael Mitchell	Karen Murphy
Alicia Lewis	Karen Manchester	Suzanne McCullagh	Renauld Mitchell	Rory Murphy
Jacob Lewis	Linda Manering	Carla McDaniels	Signora Mitchell	Sarah Murphy
Kathryn Lewis	Albert Manetta	Loren McDonald	Tami Miyahara	Shannon Murphy
Monique Lewis	Camran Mani	Katherine McGee	Norrell Mizera	Grace Murray

John Murray
Patrice Murtha
Allison Muscolino
Meghan Musolff
Antonio Mussari
Barbara Myles
Allison Nadeau
Anthony Nakvosas
Kevin Nason
Andrew Natale
John Neal
Elizabeth Neely
Reginald Neely
Jane Neet
Adam Nelson
Dona Nelson
Jordan Nelson
Ruth Nelson
Samuel Nelson
Sarah Nelson
Stephanie Nelson
Martha Neth
Susie Newman
Aaron Newton
Xuan Ming Ng
Chi Nguyen
Kimberly Nichols
Thea Nichols
Natasha Nickodem
Michael Nicolai
Emily Nieder
Sarah Niedzwiecki
Christina Nielsen
Kristine Nielsen
Jeffrey Nigro
Cynthia Noble
Janine Nock
James Nocon
Ashley Noel
Pamela Nogales
Guadalupe Noguez
Jude Nolen
Geoffrey Norfleet
Bruce Norman
Brittany Norment
Christina Normore
Leigh Norris
Matthew Norris
Jacqueline Norton
Jaime Norwood

Gregory Nosan
Bradley Nowak
Linda Nowak
Randall Nufer
Rogelio Nunez
Caroline Nutley
Oswald Nyepan
Brian Oberhauser
Jennifer Oberhauser
Monica Obniski
Rene Justin Ocampo
James Ochs
Thomas O'Connell
Gardiner O'Kain
Elvee O'Kelley
Dana Oliveri
Daniel Oljaca
MaryEl Olliffe
Pamela Ollison
Julia Olsen
Madeleine Olsen
Kristine O'Reilly
Sarah Oremland
Daniel Orendorff
Sheryl Orlove
Curtis Osmun
Antonio Otero
Zachariah Overley
Heather Owens
Kathleen Oyervides
Susan Packard
Joanne Pagan
Lindsay Page
Neysa Page-Lieberman
Jose Palermo
David Palmer
Gojko Pamucar
Dimitrios Panagopoulos
Thomas Panka
Melanie Pankau
Jennifer Paoletti
Emilia Pappas
Antonette Paraiso
Kara Parham
Hyun Joo Park
Jocelyn Park
Alana Parker
Janet Parker
Rebecca Parker
Nathaniel Parks

Wayne Parthun
Lea Pascal
Mark Pascale
Katherin Pasquith
Kaushalya Patel
Brittany Patterson
Mary Patton
Karin Patzke
Ryan Paveza
Kim Paymaster
Renee Payne
Carla Paynter
Clo Pazera
Elinor Pearlstein
Darryl Pearson
April Peck
Maria Peinado
Audrey Peiper
Susan Pellowe
Amy Peltz
Theresa Penland
Smitha Pennepalli
Nadine Pennypacker
Ivan Perez
Jessica Perez
Leon Perez
Felicia Perkins
Katrina Perkins
Mary Lou Perkins
Phillip Perkins
Voncia Perkins
Chauncey Perry
Corelle Perry
LaFrancine Perry
Katharine Perutz
Therese Peskowits
Michelle Pestlin
James Peterson
Kevin Peterson
Jessica Petertil
Tina Phan
Jeremy Phillips
Julius Phillips
Leotha Phillips
Damar Phyfiher
Kristina Piedra
Camilla Pietrabissa
Charles Pietraszewski
Diana Pilipenko
Luis Pimentel

Joanna Pineda
Ana Pita
Jessica Pittenger
James Pittman
Marjorie Pitts
Martin Plesha
Sarah Plumb
Barbara Podgornik
Robert Polachek
Rebecca Pollak
Denise Pollentier
Elizabeth Pope
Sarah Pope
Bethanne Portala
Joshua Porter
Taylor Poulin
Mary Katherine Powell
Sandhya Prakash
Carol Preacely
Aay Preston-Myint
Jeremy Price
Daniel Pride
Karen Pride
Pamela Prosch
Caitlin Prouty
Ricky Pruitt
Luke Przybylski
Maureen Pskowski
Mack Pulliam
Debra Purden
Tara Quell
Samuel Quigley
Aza Quinn-Brauner
Valente Quintero
Amy Radick
Sarah Raettig
Kathryn Rahn
George Rakar
Tori Ramey
Brenda Ramirez
Esther Ramirez
Michelle Ramirez
Raymond Ramirez
Divya Rao
Kevin Rapp
Robert Rasmussen
Justin Rathell
Marianne Rathslag
Paris Ratliff
Brent Raymond

Michal Raz-Russo
Allister Redd
Carolyn Reddy
Rita Redfield
Susan Reed
Leslie Reese
Carmen Reeves
Dianna Reeves
Dane Rehner
Katherine Reilly
Robert Reinard
Patricia Relford
Patricia Repp
Christopher Retana
Michelle Revelt
Gregory Reyes
Robert Reynolds
Barbara Rhodes
Melissa Rias
Nora Riccio
Robert Ricker
Timothy Ridlen
Sadieh Rifai
Rachel Riffel
Charles Riley
Thomas Riley
David Rini
Shannon Riordan
Consuelo Rios De Mendez
Abraham Ritchie
Isabel Rivera
Joseph Rivera
Melissa Rivera
Richard Rizzo
Anne Roberts
Ellen Roberts
Morgan Roberts
Nicole Roberts
Sharhonda Roberts
Jillian Robinson
Mary Robinson
William Robinson, Jr.
Robert Roblin
Lillian Roby
Rosie Roche
Houston Roderick
John Rodgers
Joanna Rodriguez
Nelida Rodriguez
Thelma Rodriguez

Miguel Rodriguez, Jr.
Alecia Rogers
Irene Rogers
Margaret Rogers
Patrick Rogers
Rita Rogers
Andre Rollins
Catherine Roman
Joseph Roman
Katherine Romano
Tony Romano
David Romero
Marisa Romo
James Rondeau
Joseph Rosa
Clare Rosean
Heather Roseberry
Marilyn Rosengarden
Charita Ross
Tanya Ross
Susan Rossen
Molly Roth
Tricia Rowland-Walton
Sarah Royston
Monica Rubalcava-Zuniga
Caitlin Rubin
Miguel Rubio
Carrie Ruckel
Rebecca Ruderman
Ivan Ruiz
Josefina Ruiz
Tricia Rumbolz
Keith Rupert
Emily Rutter
Brandon Ruud
Maureen Ryan
Zoë Ryan
Bart Ryckbosch
Kathleen Ryczek
Matthew Saba
Vergel Saez
Becky Saiki
Brandon Salmans
Britany Salsbury
Gregory Sampson
Terry Sampson
Kimberly Samson
Shawn Samuels
Jose Sanchez
Victoria Sanchez

Christopher Sanders
Hannah Sanders
John Sanford
Joseph Sangster
Jonita Sapp
Vanessa Saran
Abigail Satinsky
Gregory Sato
Anne Sautman
Katherine Scafidi
Patricia Scanlan
Lelia Scheaua
Mordecai Scheckter
Robert Schevitz
Sarah Schiff
Victoria Schiffman
Kurt Schleicher
Rebecca Schlesinger
Cher Schneider
George Schneider
Suzanne Schnepp
Robin Schnur
Devin Schoff
Katherine Schofield
Lauren Schreiber
Dorothy Schroeder
Samantha Schroeder
Stacey Schroeder
Eva-Maria Schuchardt
Maria Schulman
Lauren Schultz
Steven Schwark
Michal Schwartz
Sarah Schwartz
Zoe Schwartz
Christopher Scott
Darin Scott
David Scott
Mary Scott
Regina Scott
Victoria Scott
Samuel Scranton
Catherine Scully
Michael Searcy
Margaret Sears
Lawrence Seaton
Kimberly Seger
Holly Seibel
Betty Seid
Patricia Semeniuk

Peter Semeniuk
Salvatore Seminara
Chelsea Seramur
Christina Serrato
Douglas Severson
Rex Sexton
Harlan Seyton
George Sferra III
Amira Shabana
Lisa Shabez
Sarah Shaheen
Jocelin Shalom
Laurie Shaman
Robert Sharp
Jill Shaw
Jeremy Shelton
Christopher Shepherd
Tyler Sherman
Daniel Sherry
Melanie Sherwinski
Kathleen Sherwood
Yini Shi
Melissa Shinall
Elizabeth Shingleton
Yaregal Shita
Elisa Shoenberger
Marshall Shord
Jonathan Shultz
Ryan Shuquem
Helga Siebert
Jessica Siebert
Elizabeth Siegel
Rana Siegel
Jennifer Siering
Amanda Signore
Bobbie Sihere
Donna Silverman
Merle Silverstein
Julie Simek
Claire Simmons
Jevoid Simmons
Lee Simmons
Melissa Simo
Maria Simon
Michael Sims
Debra Singleton
Tamekia Singleton
Samantha Singley
Jill Sison
Katherine Skaggs

Margaret Skimina
Jeffrey Skoblar
Andrew Skomra
Roberta Skufca Kenealy
Hannah Slater
Mark Slima
Jerri Smart
Yelizaveta Smirnova
Aaron Smith
Adelaide Smith
Angela Smith
Clairellyn Smith
Clinton Smith
Hilary Smith
Jermaine Smith
Kelvin Smith
Levi Smith
Melissa Smith
Newell Smith
Patrick Smith
Rashida Smith
Susan Smolinski
Irene Snead
Andrea Sokell
Graciela Solis
Luis Solis
Mary Solt
Yoon Son
Jennifer Sostaric
Emily Soszko
Jean Sousa
Travis Southworth
Tess Sparkman
Lamont Spencer
David Spiegel
Judith Spies
Gretchen Spittler
Mirja Spooner
Samantha Springer
Larry Squalls
Shante Square
Maarten Florian Staab
Margaret Staab
Linda Stack
Karyn Stafford
Agnes Starczewski
David Stark
Paul Stauffer
Jason Stec
Sarah Steckel

Theresa Steenwyk
Lorien Steere
Melinda Stefanski
David Stempowski
Amanda Stenlund
Charles Stephens
Mary Suzanne Stephens
Elizabeth Stephenson
Elizabeth Stepina
Barry Steptore
Anika Sterba
Megan Sterling
Dana Stewart
Lyslie Stewart
Michael Stewart
Shenelda Stewart-Evans
Carla Stillwell
James Stinehelfer
Krystal Stoelting
Louis Stokes
Marvin Stokes
Matthew Stolle
Courtney Stone
Gary Stoppelman
Harriet Stratis
Zarina Stroger
Paige Strohmaier
Myroslava Struk
Ann Stuart
Gregory Stuart
Benjamin Stuber
Dottie Ann Stucko
Molly Sturdevant
Annie Sturgis
Carol Suero-Leahy
Alix Sugarman
Ann Sugg
Joan Sullivan
Kathryn Sullivan
Leonard Sullivan
Susie Sutton
Hannah Swartz
Rebecca Swayze
Marilynn Sweeney
Timothy Swezy
Marisa Swystun
Belinda Sykes
Lawrence Sykes
Alisa Symonds
Katharine Sytsma

Michael Szymczak	Richard Townsend	Jeremiah Voeks	Ruben White	Leslie Wong
James Szyskowski	Quoc Tran	Lauren Vollono	Aura Whitfield	Daisy Wood
Charles Talbot	David Travis	Valerie Von Der Malsburg	Leisel Whitlock	Raymond Woodruff
Joseph Tallarico	Walton Treadwell	Guyla Von Moore	Mark Wielgosinski	Laura Woods
Chalida Tangsurat	Tanya Treptow	Olga Vucinic	Kenneth Wiese	Milton Woods
Lucia Tantardini Lloyd	Nikhil Trivedi	Kirk Vuillemot	Kamilah Willard	Patricia Woodworth
Raymond Tapia	Brian Truex	Catherine Wagner	Brittany Williams	Mary Woolever
Monique Tarleton	Jann Trujillo	Awal Wahab	Jason Williams	James Wooters
Frank Tassone	Nicole Trumpinski	Kristen Wahl	Kenneth Williams	Patrick Wozny
Albert Taylor	Gregory Tschann	Leslie Wakeford	Linda Williams	Martha Wright
Brian Taylor	Bruce Tulloch	Christopher Walenga	Maggie Williams	Faye Wrubel
Delores Taylor	Jennifer Tullock	Anna Walker	Markus Williams	Jie Xu
Garland Taylor	Vivien Tung	Brittany Walker	Michelle Williams	Debra Yarnell
Jade Taylor	Veronica Turpin	George Walker, Jr.	Quentessa Williams	Agnieszka-Anna Yass
Jessica Taylor	Courtney Uchytil	David Walksler	Rebecca Williams	Gilbert Yates
Lara Taylor	Richard Uecker	Jeff Walls	Reina Williams	Sze Sze Yockey
Sara Taylor	Leah Ujda	Jerico Walls	Russell Williams	Tamra Yost
Gloria Taylor-Davenport	John Ulrich	Donna Walters	Trebour Williams	Brandon Young
Martha Tedeschi	Jose Unzueta	Christopher Wanklyn	Vanessa Williams	John Young
Katherine Teed	De'Andre Upshaw	Benjamin Ward	Loretha Willis	Nicholas Young
Jennifer Teixiera	Sara Urizar	Catherine Ward	Imelda Willsmer	Ronald Young
Catharine Telfair	Bruce Valdes	Christine Ward	Francesca Wilmott	Christopher Yovich
Brendan Telzrow	Jennifer Valdez	Tina Ward	Arion Wilson	George Yovkovich
Pilar Tena	Alexander Valentine III	Meghan Warkentin	Corinne Wilson	Michael Yunk
Earl Terry	Georgina Valverde	Emily Warner	David Wilson	Amy Zavaleta
Jennifer Thielen	Lori Van Deman Iseri	Fern Warshell	Frank Wilson	Peter Zegers
Camille Thigpen	Julia van den Hout	Kyle Waterman	Marie Wilson	Alicja Zelazko
Camille Thomas	Ray Van Hook	Alberta Watkins	Matthew Wilson	Peter Zelenski
Ericka Thomas	Sarah Van Pelt	Deborah Watkins	Melvin Wilson	Ghenete Zelleke
Fallon Thomas	Anthony Van Winkle	Brian Watson	Valerie Wilson	Beatriz Zengotitabengoa
Imogene Thomas	Crystal VanDeCasteele	Kimberly Watt	William Windham	Li Dong Zhang
Leisa Thomas	Joel Vanderkamp	Coretta Webb	Haily Wineland	Carolyn Ziebarth
Mon Thomas	Kim Vandevoorde	Deborah Webb	Anthony Winfield	Emily Ziemba
Shanté Thomas	Seth Vanek	Kurt Weber	Pearl Winford	Patricia Zirbel
Tiya Thomas	Lauren Varga	Cecile Webster	Abigail Winograd	Stephen Zirbel
Courtney Thompson	Joseph Vatinno	Susan Weidemeyer	Adam Winston	Dzenan Zisko
Leonard Thompson	Falicia Vaughn	William Weinand	Paula Wisotzki	Jasminka Zisko
Sandra Thompson	Leticia Velazquez	Nicolas Weise	Lindsey Wisz	Frank Zuccari
Julie Thomson	Marco Velazquez	Gregory Weiss	Asha Witherspoon	Flavia Zuniga-West
Garnet Thorne	Rafael Vellos	Andrew Weissmann	Matthew Witkovsky	Rachel Zupek
Martha Thorne	Lucio Ventura	Kathryn Wellington	Mary Witte	Samantha Zwiebel
Emily Thornton	Sally Venverloh	Aaron Wells	Susan Wojcik	
Kathleen Thornton	José Versoza III	Nanette Wells	Julia Wolf	
Christa Thurman	Karin Victoria	Jennifer Welsing	Michael Wolf	
Gary Tibor	Anna Vila Espuna	Hilary Wentz	Sabina Wolf	
Kimberly Tidwell	Yadira Villa	Erik Wenzel	Thomas Wolfe	
Adam Torres	Christine Villanueva	Jeffrey Wertheimer	Martha Wolff	
Angelica Torres	Ronnie Virden	Lena West	Jeffrey Wonderland	
Philip Toscano	Hugh Visor	Mary Whedbee	Candice Wong	
Lars Townsend	Virginia Voedisch	Reginald White	Caryn Wong	

PROJECT PERSONNEL FOR THE MODERN WING AND THE NICHOLS BRIDGEWAY

THE ART INSTITUTE
OF CHICAGO
James Cuno
Meredith Mack
Douglas Druick
Stephanie D'Alessandro
James Rondeau
Joe Rosa
Matt Witkovsky
Robert Eskridge

DESIGN ARCHITECT
*Renzo Piano Building
Workshop*
Renzo Piano
Joost Moolhuijzen
Dominique Rat
Carolyn Maxwell-Mahon

ARCHITECT OF RECORD
Interactive Design, Inc.
Robert Larsen
Charles G. Young
Dina Griffin

LANDSCAPE ARCHITECT
Gustafson Guthrie Nichol Ltd.
Jennifer Guthrie
Kathryn Gustafson

MECHANICAL,
ELECTRICAL, PLUMBING,
STRUCTURAL ENGINEER
Arup
Andy Sedgwick
Bob Lang

PROGRAM MANAGER
The Rise Group, LLC
Leif Selkregg
Barry Quinn
Bridget Bush
Rick Watson

SITE CIVIL
ENGINEERING—
MODERN WING
Patrick Engineering, Inc.

SITE CIVIL
ENGINEERING—
NICHOLS BRIDGEWAY
H. W. Lochner

COMMISSIONING AND
LEED CONSULTING
Carter & Burgess

ELECTRICAL
ENGINEERING
CONSULTING
Jose de Avila and Associates

MECHANICAL
ENGINEERING
CONSULTING
Sebesta Blomberg
and Associates

STRUCTURAL
ENGINEERING AND
VIBRATION MONITORING
CONSULTING
Wiss Janney Elstner
Associates, Inc.

AUDIOVISUAL
CONSULTING
The Talaske Group

SECURITY CONSULTING
Sako

VERTICAL
TRANSPORTATION
CONSULTING
Jenkins and Huntington

RETAIL CONSULTING
Charles Sparks and
Company

KITCHEN/CAFE
CONSULTING
Aria Group Architects

PROJECT ESTIMATING
Morgan Construction
Consultants, Inc.

MBE/WBE CONSULTING
The Target Group

SIGNAGE DESIGN
Pentagram
Entro Communications

RESTAURANT DESIGN
Dirk Denison Architects

CONSTRUCTION
TESTING
ECS, Ltd.

THE MODERN WING /
NICHOLS BRIDGEWAY
CONSTRUCTION TEAM
Construction Manager
Turner Construction
Company
  Greg Mulac
  Nick Canellis
  Steve Fort

*Building Excavation,
Earth Retention, and
Foundations*
Brandenburg Industrial
Hayward Baker Inc.
Case Foundations

Structural Steel
Construction Systems, Inc.

Structural Steel Erection
Area Erectors

Concrete
Tribco Construction
Services, LLC

Mechanical Systems
Hill Mechanical
Corporation

*Mechanical Systems
Testing and Balance*
Professional Systems
Analysis, Inc.

Plumbing
Barry Thomas Plumbing Inc.

*Building Electrical and
Low-Voltage Systems*
Continental Electrical
Construction Company, LLC

Enabling Electrical Work
Gibson Electric &
Technology Solutions

*High-Voltage Electrical
Installation*
Meade Electric
Company, Inc.

Architectural Precast Beams
Lombard Architectural
Precast

*Curtainwall, Skylights, and
Flying Carpet*
Josef Gartner USA

Exterior Limestone
W. R. Weis Company, Inc.

Wood Flooring
P. J. Nagic, Inc.

Ceilings
Airtite, Inc.

Rough Carpentry
Edwin Anderson
Construction Company

Drywall and Plaster
R. G. Construction
Services, Inc.

*Shades and Miscellaneous
Accessories*
Interior Concepts, Inc.

Coatroom Equipment
Railex Corporation

Interior Glazed Partitions
Harmon, Inc.

Fire Protection Systems
Wolverine Fire Protection
Company

Elevators
Mitsubishi Electric &
Electronics USA, Inc.

Escalator
Montgomery Kone

Architectural Millwork
Imperial Woodworking
Company

Ceramic Tile
Premier Tile & Stone, LLC

Carpet and VCT
Kingston Tile Company, Ltd.

Painting
Continental Painting &
Decorating, Inc.

Fireproofing
Spray Insulation

*Doors, Frames, and
Hardware*
LaForce
Door Systems
Modernfold Doors

Balanced Doors
MTH Industries

Food Service Equipment
M. L. Rongo
TriMark Marlinn

Security Installation
Honeywell

Audiovisual Installation
Pentegra Systems

Retail Shop
J. R. Jones Fixture Company

Moveable Gallery Partitions
kub2

Gallery Lighting
Lighting Services, Inc.

Roofing
All American Exterior
Solutions

Miscellaneous Metals
Meccor Industries, Ltd.

Landscape
Christy Webber
Landscapes

Site Waterproofing
Sager Sealants

Building Insulation
Superl Inc.

Building Control Systems
Johnson Controls, Inc.

Exhibition Casework
EDE Corporation
Proto Productions

Furniture
Henricksen
Interior Investments
OM Workspace

Project Signage
Nordquist Sign Company
Accessories Plus, Inc.

Restaurant Buildout
Turner Construction
Company,
Special Projects Division

*Nichols Bridgeway
Fabrication*
Industrial Steel Construction

Nichols Bridgeway Erection
Danny's Construction
Company, Inc.

*Nichols Bridgeway Metal
Deck / Snowmelt Systems*
Bayards Aluminium
Construction

Nichols Bridgeway Concrete
Schaefges Brothers, Inc.

*Nichols Bridgeway
Excavation*
John Keno and
Company, Inc.

Nichols Bridgeway Painting
DBM Services

*Nichols Bridgeway
Waterproofing*
Kedmont Waterproofing

*Nichols Bridgeway Site
Concrete*
Martin Cement

And a very special thanks
on the Nichols Bridgeway
to Lou Kulekowskis.

PROJECT DATA

Project design
1999–2005

Groundbreaking
May 31, 2005

Project construction
2005–2009

Building dedication
May 16, 2009

Gross surface
264,000 square feet

Exhibition space
64,000 square feet

Education space
20,000 square feet

Cost
$294,000,000

Exterior materials
Indiana limestone, glass,
steel, and aluminum

Interior materials
Glass, plaster walls,
white oak flooring, and
birch and cherry accents